Y0-AJL-422

North Carolina
MOUNTAIN FOLKLORE
And Miscellany

• • •

By HORTON COOPER

• • •

Copyright 1972 by
JOHNSON PUBLISHING COMPANY
Murfreesboro, N. C. 27855

Wingate College Library

Dedicated to
MINNIE
Forever a lover of the North Carolina Mountains and their people.

Contents

Preface	5
Old Mountaineer	8
Mountain Medicine	9
How Dear to Our Hearts the Memories	19
Folklore Trails of the Mountains	28
In the Old Days	35
The Wake	39
The Linebeck Ghost	45
The Ghosts of Whispering Creek	48
The Ghosts of Yellow Mountain Gap	50
Tongue Twisters	53
Riddles	55
Those Seasons Long Ago	57
Folk Bible Questions	60
Children's Games and Pastimes	61
Weather Wisdom	64
General Superstitions	69
Old Superstitions Regarding Animals	71
Old Superstitions Once Were Not Superficial	72
Magic Formulas	77
Children's Rhymes	82
Misquotations from Scripture	86
The Early Vernacular of the N. C. Mountains	87
An Old-Timey Sparkin'	98
Proverbs and Expressions	101
Early School Rules	102
Old Popular Songs and Ballads	106
Yates Radford, Typical Mountaineer	115
The Tuckahoes	123
Old Superstitions	137

MISCELLANY

Grandfather Mountain	142
The Answers	144

Early Life in the North Carolina Mountains 145
The Anthology of Death 148
Why Not Come Over and Borrow? 150
Colorful Place Names 151
Funny Incidents 152
With Love to Beautiful Western North Carolina 154
I Want to Go Back 157

• • •

Folklore

FOLKLORE: "The traditions, beliefs, customs, etc. of a people." —*Webster's Dictionary.*

"Folklore is that complex knowledge (beliefs, customs, magic, sayings, songs, tales, traditions, and so on) which has been created by spontaneous play of naive imaginations upon common human experience, transmitted by word of mouth or action, and preserved without dependence upon written or printed record."
—*Arthur Palmer Hudson.*

"Mountain folklore is truly a way of life, and the way of life in the mountains naturally breeds lore."
—*John Parris.*

Preface

THIS book grew out of my having lived in and traveled the length and breadth of the North Carolina mountain area for more than eighty years, loving the people and absorbing the wealth of folklore which the mountains bred. While it contains much that is as old as the coming of the first pioneers, a great deal of it has originated and existed for generations since in the beautiful highland region.

Being a mountaineer and proudly grateful of it, all my life I have been interested in the wealth of folklore that the mountains have bred. The first folklore I remember having heard consisted of rhymes, jingles and ditties recited in my mother's arms at bedtime, when I was sleepy; much of it came from my maternal grandfather; my boyhood and adult companions handled bits of it; and almost wherever I went, soon or late, others would use some of the old traditions and sayings, utter one of the proverbs, sing an old ballad or tell an exciting story. Although the old folk talk was slowly becoming extinct in my early manhood, it was often spoken, and much of it lingered on the lips and tongues of my friends for decades afterward. In some isolated places, it has not yet entirely vanished. I *picked up* much of the old vernacular from many of the pupils I taught, their parents and neighbors.

All mountaineers have always liked a good legend, ghost story, ballad or picturesque expression, but a big segment of the population never took seriously the old superstitions which others accepted and allowed to have profound influence on their lives.

Although some sensational writers from outside the area have pictured the North Carolina mountaineer of the past as ignorant, illiterate and lazy, the fact is that as a whole he was no more uninformed, illiterate or less industrious than the average in the lowlands. His planning, industry and success in overcoming what at first was a harsh environment bears the truth of this statement. When the Civil War ended and the South lay like a wounded goddess, the curtain had fallen upon most of the rural regions of the State and for decades the real imagination and aggressiveness of the mountaineer were displayed to such an extent that, more quickly than in most areas, recovery came sooner. The old economic and social order regained itself and surged forward at a rapid rate, for forced labor had never been a factor in its growth.

The pioneers, much to their honor, brought their Bibles with them and built churches almost as soon as they built homes. Without good schools and other media of literary knowledge, studying Scripture caused them to hold to the belief that the world is flat, and this belief was entertained by many of their descendants for decades.

The people of the North Carolina mountains are mainly of English and Scotch-Irish descent, with Anglo-Saxon predominating, although there are mixtures of German, Dutch and Welsh. As a rule, the Latin races shunned the highlands. They have been characterized by self-reliance. Iniative, aggressiveness and rugged individualism have aided them in establishing, almost from the first, an almost self-sufficient economy that fit their culture and social structure to a challenging environment. The language of the first-comers and their descendants for many decades was that of the Elizabethans and it clung to their lips in Shakespeare and Chaucer flavor, along with a racy, colorful dialect which had originated in the mountains. Schools and colleges, a wealth of libraries, radio and television and excellent communication with the outside world have caused the colorful dialect to fade almost to the vanishing point.

Superstition was not pecular to the mountain people. All the earth has regional superstition, although with many, greatly hidden, it lies near the surface. United States presidents have been known to have pet superstitions and many actors and actresses today entertain them. They originate from experiences of life.

The mountains now are as close to Raleigh as the coastal dunes or the Sandhills or the Albemarle. The automobile and the new highways bring them all within a day's range, and the isolation which once characterized mountain life has gone the way of the log cabin and the buggy. Still, the memory of the past lingers in the hills, even as it does on the plains, and the history of the mountain country is rich with the spirit of America.

In the honey haze of nostalgia, the memories have become as dear to the heart as the names in the family Bible and as bright as the lamps of Grandpa's buggy.

Our appreciation is extended to the Asheville *Citizen-Times* for use of illustrations on pages 20, 153 and 160 and to the Raleigh *News and Observer* for use of illustrations on pages 10, 42 and 76. Additional illustrations are from March 1875 *Harper's Monthly* magazine and other late Nineteenth Century publications. We are indebted to Mr. and Mrs. Gurney Franklin, Robert (Bob) Franklin and Mrs. Artie G. Laws for the rare photographs on pages 161-168.

—*Horton Cooper.*

Old Mountaineer

LONG are the years I have lived in the mountains,
   The years that have hurried my youth-time away.
I know what language the four seasons whisper;
I know what the wind and breezes say.
I've walked the bright road where April was passing;
I've thrilled to October with gladness and wonder;
I know what will heal men of *tizick* and fever
I know where the red fox has denned up yonder.

I've never been away from here—never have wandered—
Never got going to lands far away,
For I've drunk the cold water, I'm bound to the hills here,
And here in the mountains is where I shall stay.
The old hills have told me the things that I know well,
So I shall sleep peacefully here when I go
To my last bed, while the soft wind is sighing;
I shall sleep well where these cold waters flow.

1
Mountain Medicine

THE early doctors of the Carolina Mountains were, as a rule, highly esteemed, for they had ideas. They cooked up things.

They had attended no medical or pharmacy schools, nor had any recognized authority issued them licenses or diplomas. But in the absence or scarcity of real druggists or physicians, they tried faithfully to make well again those who suffered from disease or hurt. Many of them succeeded remarkably well. Numerous patients recovered, while some were tuck, but everyone knew that, in the last analysis, death always won the final round.

The doctors flourished in the rural areas and small towns from the coming of the first settlers until after the turn of the century, but even now in scattered communities a few still attend the sick. Despite their serious lack of medical knowledge, they were the answer to the problem of illness and injury, childbirth and aching teeth in an isolated region where trained practitioners were not available.

Their kind did not originate in the mountains, for there were those from early colonial days in lowlands and among the hills who were relied upon in time of illness to relieve suffering. Society, wherever human beings lived, expected and demanded special knowledge of a few which could cope with the inevitable human ills as they came.

Trained physicians, surgeons and nurses first came to the Carolina lowlands, where population encouraged their practice with greater remuneration. Slowly home remedies and the formulas for the specially skilled were

Families relied on Nature's drug store.

forgotten, while in the Appalachian Mountains, where existed the richest flora of the temperate zone outside of Japan, the many medicinal plants and the scarcity of real physicians created a situation which encouraged those who were medically inclined to expermient and learn how to be of service to their fellow citizens.

Long after trained physicians had established themselves miles apart, these old doctors did a thriving business, for they could be reached more quickly, their fees fitted the poor man's pocketbook, many families were skeptical of new-fangled medicines and the old practitioners had earned reputations which continued to merit reliance when troubles came.

Nature opened the first drugstore and because man was constantly on the move, nature's drugstore had branches everywhere. The aborigines were aware of this and depended upon its stock of herbs, roots and barks for curative results. For many generations, every mountaineer recognized the curative principles of many crude drugs and was more or less his own physician in many illnesses, especially the minor ones. But relatively few had the time in which to accumulate an extensive knowledge of the curative properties of the many crude drugs that grew in abundance all about them; to mix and blend the ingredients of salves, tinctures and infusions; to learn the art of extracting aching teeth; and to learn the formulas, if available, for magic treatment.

There had to be specialists who devoted a great deal of their time to gathering and experimenting with the many crude drugs and who had the patience to produce pure medicines in their laboratories, consisting mainly of pots, pans, troughs and earthen jars. There had to be available storage space for the many crude drugs which would be turned into medicines. Anyone could treat a common cold, but few could recognize and treat pneumonia and the most dreaded diseases.

The virtue of decoctions, infusions, tinctures, distillations, salves and poultices were highly respected, and rightly so, for many doctors of the mountains produced some medicines which almost equaled in remedial principles those used by real physicians of the time in the largest cities of the Tar Heel lowlands. Despite this fact, the best available medicines then, as today, were unable to produce the results wished for and it was then that magic and witchcraft played their colorful parts in many cases.

There were those who called themselves Old Indian Herb Doctors, claiming that they had learned the virtues and preparation of crude drugs from the Indians. Most of them had never seen an Indian. Too, there were a few Spanish Herb Doctors, Vegetable Doctors and lots of Neighborhood Herb Doctors. All possessed a knowledge of simple remedies that were not without their value. Even the limited medical knowledge of these self-styled doctors plus the native crude drug preparations plus the willingness shown in a devotion to the alleviation of pain were unquestionably of great good when illness came and no other source of medical help was available.

The doctors had obtained their meager medical knowledge from various sources. A part of it had been handed down from father to son for many generations. Some of it consisted of Indian lore, a portion of it was the result of the trial and error method and much of it was a carry-over from a European setting.

Knowing some of the properties of medicine and that the action of a remedy upon the human system depends upon attributes peculiar to it, they used hot infusions of catnip, dog-fennel, ginger, boneset, sage, butterfly weed and snakeroot as sudorifics for prducing sweating in the treatment of measles, colds, grippe and pneumonia. Yellow dock, mandrake, poke root, blood root and black cohosh were used as alternatives to tone up the system and establish a healthy condition. They made these into both decoctions and tinctures.

Some of them, at least, understood that alternatives may possess tonic, stimulant, laxative or diuretic properties all combined in one remedy and they combined them in various ways.

The last Old Spanish Herb Doctor of the Carolina Mountains, as far as is known, left the state forty-seven years ago. He made anodynes to relieve pain by blunting the sensibility of the nerves from poppies grown in his flower garden, Deadly Nightshade from the fields, and the herb herbane. He used hops as a remedy for wakefulness; worm medicine was made from the seeds of the vermifudge (Old Jerusalem) plant, which had been introduced into the mountains by the early settlers; tonics were made from wild cherry bark and stone root; and queen's root and Stillinga were for common colds.

As they became available, calomel, quinine and camphor were used extensively by most of the self-styled doctors in the treatment of various diseases.

The Honey And Brandy Doctors claimed to know the exact amount of honey and brandy to be mixed, the size and timing of the doses, and the length of treatment required to cure a case of milk sick or milk poison.

This malady was caused by the use of milk, butter or flesh of an animal which had eaten a variety of white snakeroot herb when the pastures were low because of drought. The ailment caused nausea, vomiting, dizziness and extreme prostration as the disease progressed. Often death resulted.

None knew then what caused the illness and until Purdue University of Indiana discovered the origin it was thought that a poisonous dew or gas had settled upon the vegetation during late summer. So prevalent was this strange malady that a book was written calling it *the Great Scourge of the Appalachians*. In most cases the patient recovered, because the honey and brandy treatment apparently had *killed* the poison, but physicians today declare that the remedy was not only valueless, but extremely dangerous.

Rheumatiz Doctors had many remedies, many of which could be administered by the patient or members of his family. Sometimes stones were heated, wrapped in cloths or pelts and applied to the aching joints and muscles. Often patients were advised to carry buckeyes in the pocket.

Occasionally the sufferer was made to carry a potato for months in his pocket, the cure coming after the potato had become stone-hard and was said to be petrified. Bee stings, snake poison and snake oil were administered by the practitioner, but they had no real curative values beyond their psychological effect. The patient's joints were bathed for hours daily with vinegar and hot water or a mixture of grease, turpentine and kerosene. Later, bracelets of copper wire were worn on the wrist.

The midwife, known as the granny womern, was one of the most indispensable persons of the community. She generally relied upon the practical knowledge gained over the years as a helper, but she was not averse to using odd remedies and magic formulas when she believed their use was justified.

To induce a quick delivery, she held powdered tobacco leaves or snuff under the patient's nose to produce sneezing. This was known as snuffing the patient. She fumed and fretted when the birth was not occurring within a week before or or after fullmoon. Sometimes she placed an axe under the patient's bed to cut the pains and time of delivery.

She held herslf in readiness to answer a call anywhere in her area, regardless of the hour, day or night, the distance or the weather conditions. When possible, she rode horseback, but often she tramped rough paths over the mountains, waded creeks and rivers and sometimes used her own body as a bulldozer when encountering snowdrifts.

Occasionally she received money for her services, but more often her fees were paid in such things as ginseng roots, cured pork, chickens, leather and the fruit of the loom. She expected nothing from the poorer families. In her fervor to serve her neighbors she was content in knowing that all she had cotch belonged to the rare breed of men who lived in the Appalachian Mountains of North Carolina and who would grow up to be tall in the sight of God.

Besides the business of catching babies, she was often consulted regarding simple remedies which other medics apparently had overlooked. She advised putting sulphur on a chronic sore, tieing a yarn thread around a cracked toe, smearing a badly chapped thumb with white pine rosin and using fresh cow dung to cure a boil. She treated cramp colic—probably gall bladder colic or appendicitis—with a decoction of dried tobacco stems. And she always kept a supply of stalls—cloth or leather protective shields or sheaths—for sore thumbs and fingers.

The tooth-puller and the tooth-jumper were known as Tooth Doctors. Decayed and aching teeth were usually tolerated for a long while before most persons overcame their timidity sufficiently to have them extracted.

The pain was treated in the home by holding a bag of hot ashes on the jaw or cheek, holding cold water on the aching tooth for several minutes, plastering the cavity with snuff, smoking a corncob pipe filled with homemade tobacco until vomiting occurred, drinking a few snorts of peartenin' juice or picking the tooth with a splinter from a tree which had been struck by lightning. When neuralgia struck, peartenin' juice was sipped until one could not walk a crack in the floor.

When worse came to worst, either the tooth-puller or the tooth-jumper was visited for the tooth to be extracted. In either case the patient would be given two or three good drinks of brandy or whisky and allowed to wait until the distilled spirits overcame the timidity of his own spirit.

If a tooth-puller was performing the rough work, the patient was made to lie upon the floor or ground, and the crude doctor of dental surgery knelt astride him, forceps in hand. Often the aching tooth was yanked out during what appeared to be a wrestling match as the determined tooth-puller performed the task allotted him.

The tooth-jumper was usually an expert who completed his job quickly. A hammer and a chisel about the size of a fairly large nail were used. The chisel was placed against the tooth, just under the edge of the gum, and it was given a sharp, quick tap, which caused the tooth to jump from its socket.

Sometimes accidents happened. The jawbone was fractured or the patient was hit on the nose or chin with the hammer, usually because he moved at the wrong time. Bleeding was stopped by packing salt in the vacancy left by the tooth or the gum was rinsed with a solution of tannic acid obtained by making a decoction of oak bark.

Those who were known as Neighborhood Doctors possessed some knowledge of the medicinal properties of a few crude drugs, held to beliefs in magic remedies and prescribed odd and strange cures for common diseases, especially of children. They measured a child suffering from phthisis with a whiteoak rod and placed the rod under the eaves of a house, prescribed sheep dung tea for measles and fried onion poultices for sore throat.

Usually there was only one person — commonly a woman — in each community who had *sufficient* faith to be a Blood Doctor and able to stop profuse bleeding from nose or cut by reading or reciting in a loud, clear and confident tone to the patient the sixth verse of the Sixteenth Chapter of Ezekiel. Strange to say, the bleeding usually stopped after this verse was recited three times. Sometimes it didn't work, then crushed puffballs, spider webs and soot were applied. Cold compresses, applications of salt or ooze of oak bark and crushed green persimmons were used.

For warts, there were Wart Doctors who attempted to conjure away warts by reciting secret formulas in an inaudible voice while gently rubbing each small hard lump. Neither they nor their patients knew that these tumorous growths usually disappear of their own accord within a short time. Fire Doctors were called into the homes to blow the fire from burns and scalds by blowing their breaths repeatedly upon the injured spot while thinking of a magic verse learned under oath from another fire-blower who was on his deathbed. Thrush Doctors were men who had never seen their fathers, and they blew their breaths three times into a baby's mouth to cure the thrush.

If no real Thrush Doctors were available, it was thought that the baby's drinking a few drops of water from the shoe of a blackeyed young man would work a cure. Seventh sons of seventh sons were Cancer Doctors, who attempted to cure cancers on the exterior of the body by rubbing them with their little fingers. Madstone Doctors attempted to cure hydrophobia and remove the venom from snakebites with a small porous stone called a madstone, said to have been taken from the gallbladder of a deer. Corn And Bunion Doctors trimmed corns and bunions with sharp knives very expertly and bathed them with liquids of strange names.

As knowledge spread and learning increased, the Witch Doctor slowly passed from the scene with the going of the witches. There were few, if any, left by the end of the first decade of the Twentieth Century.

In his day, the Witch Doctor was an exalted and very important personality, for it was he who was always ready to combat the wickedness of the witches of his area, either by removing their witchery on beast or human being, or by punishing them as severely as their misdeeds warranted. He was very useful otherwise, for he taught the people how to avoid a witch's displeasure and vengeance; how they themselves might remove some of the minor witcheries; and he advised them that they could recognize the home of a witch by observing whether the sweep of the broom in that house was placed uppermost when it stood upright against the wall. He warned others never to accuse a witch by name.

He himself never mentioned the name of a suspected witch when persons or livestock were reported as being spelled, but when the imagined offense was a major one he drew her picture on a chip with a piece of charcoal, placed it in the fork of a stooping white oak tree and shot it with a silver bullet.

The Love Doctors were never numerous, but they were scattered throughout the Carolina Mountains. Like that of most of the other Doctors, their lore had originated outside the mountains and in many regions. They helped the forlorn in love by furnishing them Adam and Eve roots, John the Conqueror root, various love powders, and secret formulas to be recited at bedtime. They managed to obtain needles which had been used to sew burial clothes and sold them to unrequited male lovers to be stuck secretly into the shoes of their hearts' desires. They manufactured and sold bewitching powder to be sprinkled secretly upon the other sex.

The Hex Doctors were never numerous, but they used witchcraft aplenty, mostly among the Negroes, for hexing almost anything. Their potions, it was believed, helped the buyers to lay burdens upon the hearts of their enemies, to win courtships, to help them understand the opposite sex, to escape the visitations of ghosts, and to be successful in various undertakings.

The Horse Doctors, some of them fair veterinarians, treated not only domestic stock, but frequently human beings as well. They had picked up a limited knowledge of the simpler remedies, learned how to use splints and reset dislocations and they often performed operations on farm animals. They knew some properties of crude drugs. A seventeen-year-old youth once suffered a severe colic from eating several half-ripe apples and lay groaning in pain. Suddenly his father shouted to another son, "Sam is bad-off. Go and fetch the horse doctor."

Although they lacked the know-how of the trained physician, the mountain doctors served their communities well. Even those who used magic formulas in an effort to cure were psychologically beneficial. All together these men and women who were so great a part of the social life of that day contributed much to the rich folklore of the Carolina Appalachians.

2.
How Dear to Our Hearts the Memories

MOST of the long established social customs, the utensils and the tools of yesteryear in the North Carolina Mountains have passed into the limbo of forgotten things as new habits, better utensils and more serviceable implements have replaced them.

In a world where there is nothing so constant as change this should have been expected, but those who can remember the old days and the old ways of life sometimes have a nostalgic feeling and a half-wish that civilization had gone at a less rapid pace.

Today building a home is only one family's concern, but once it was the interest of the builder and all his neighbors within a radius of many miles, who appointed a day and joined their efforts in what was known as a house bee.

Often logs were hewn, boards riven and the entire log cabin was built and ready for occupancy between sunrise and sunset. Sometimes the work required two days. While the men worked, the women cooked and served the delicious food to the happy workmen. When the house was finished, all, including the children, joined in festive celebration.

Once the landowner cleared his *newground* with mighty axe stokes during the winter months, burning the heaped brush and leaving the logs until the invitation went out in the early spring for his neighbors to bring their families and friends and attend a *log-rolling*. Handspikes of oak had been prepared and stuck into the ground near the house for the husky men to select upon their arrival.

All day long, amid peals of laughter and good-humored

A nineteenth century cane mill.

A wood vendor at Asheville about 1900.

jesting, the logs were rolled into large heaps ready for burning. It was a good time for men to display feats of strength and the art of skillfully arranging the heaped logs.

While the children romped and played games, the women and larger girls either helped to prepare the noonday meal or engaged in a quilting party in another room.

Corn - shuckings, bean - stringings, apple - cutting and molasses-boilings came in the early autumn and were always festive occasions, when gaiety made labor exciting and thrilling. Whole families attended when the farmer husked his corn, but these other occasions were mostly for young folk. Courting couples took advantage of all, which had a very romantic atmosphere. There were mothers who came along to the night meetings to be chaperones of their daughters.. At corn-shuckings anyone finding a red ear of corn threw it at one of the opposite sex, who was authorized thereby to kiss the thrower. Often a jug of corn whiskey was hidden at the bottom of the pile of corn to further induce everyone to work faster in order to be the lucky finder, who, after taking the first drink, graciously passed it to all who would partake.

All these gatherings lasted until midnight, for, when the work was done, if there was no moon, lanterns were hung and Old Virginia Reel, to the tune of banjos and fiddles, engaged the majority, while others played games, most of them requiring kisses as rewards or penalties. Squeals of pretended embarassment or excitement often drowned out the string music.

Dancing parties, often referred to as frolics or *hoedowns*, occurred in most neighborhoods, but not in mnay homes of the neighborhood. These were held only in homes that had a room sufficiently large, after the furniture had been removed, to accomodate the dancers and musicians. Whiskey was the bane of many of these dances and sometimes the gathering turned into a rough-and-tumble affair, with fist fights and hair-pulling. Some families adopted the custom of inviting only paired couples to the dance to prevent disorder and occasionally the man of the house sat in a corner of the room with his shotgun in his arms and a knot maul at his side.

Hog killing time came with the first hard freeze and lasted until late January. Neighbor helped neighbor, even the women and children taking part. The hog died by the butt of an axe or a bullet, the carcass was soused into a barrel of scalding water heated by hot rocks, then scraped hurriedly lest the bristles should be *set*. The women carried the parts of pork into the kitchen and processed them. Tenderloin was cooked for lunch. Helping neighbors were given meat for their suppers.

When a couple was married, within a few nights it was serenaded or given a chivaree. The leader — every neighborhood had one—summoned his followers to meet him on a given night. The serenade consisted of dynamite and shotgun blasts, tootings of horns, the ringing of cowbells, beating of tin pans until the couple opened the door and invited everyone to come inside, where each one was *treated* to food, candy, cigars or drinks. Sometimes the husband was ridden on a rail and his head ducked in a creek. His wife was made to stand for a moment in a tub of cold water. Sometimes she was ridden a short distance in a wheelbarrow. Any couple not given a serenade felt that it had been slighted or insulted.

The *dumb supper* was popular. It took place on a midnight and was attended by several girls and young women. Everything was performed while the participants walked backward and with their hands behind their backs. No one spoke or whispered during the entire ceremony. When the small cake of unleavened bread and a glass of water were placed on the table and the plates set, all walked backward and took their seats, each girl leaving a vacant chair between herself and the next girl, the outside door of the kitchen having been opened wide.

It was thought, as silence reigned, the future husband of the first girl to be married would enter and sit beside her or a coffin would slide through the door and stop at the first who should die. Even a whisper would break the spell. Silently they strained their ears for the sound of a footstep. The night is full of noises and the slightest sound outside brought piercing screams from the tense girls, who dashed screaming from the room.

The very first Sunday schools lasted several hours. There was a parade ground, where the adults and children marched by twos for an hour, singing hymns and following a leader with a flag or banner. Tiring of singing, some of the marchers, especially those who were sweethearts, engaged in conversation and sometimes enjoyed a stolen kiss. Inside, the teachers read Scripture and taught. Selections from Webster's Blueback Speller were read. Lunch was spread either upon the crude benches or upon the ground.

Young men, then as now, asked for dates and dated members of the opposite sex, only it was different then.

The young man usually stepped to the girl's side and asked, "Do you love chicken?" If she was interested, her reply was yes, whereupon he offered his arm and said, "Have a wing." A negative reply caused him to walk ahead or drop behind, for the girl's answer had been, "I turn the back of my hand to you," as she actually gestured with her outspread hand. Refusing his offer was called *kicking* him, and a few girls who were asked for the first time really kicked the young man's shin, but lightly.

Grandfather, when a young man, courted Grandmother in the room in which her parents sat and he was allowed to remain until nine o'clock, but later the young man might sit in an adjoining room until the clock struck ten, when, if no sign of movement was in evidence, the young lady's mother called, "Daughter, it's bedtime." Within a few minutes, if there was no departure, the girl's father began beating his dog, which was the unmistakable sign that the young man's safety lay in flight.

Young men could be jealous in those days, as now, and they especially resented one from another community keeping company with a girl of their neighborhood. It often occurred that bands of young men in small groups, armed with long switches, placed themselves at intervals along the road which their rival would travel when returning home that night and, as the *outsider* came along, each group would *lay on* the *tea*, while he fled in the darkness or moonlight past the other waiting groups. Sometimes stones, seldom meant to hit the victim, were used instead.

After the discontinuance of the campground meetings, most rural preachers realized that the only opportunity for delivering *long-winded* sermons was to small congregations in the scattered churches of their denominations. The majority of them had little education and many could not even read or write. Their sermons had tunes, were filled with *graveyard* tales and of the fire-and-brimstone type.

It was customary that a deceased person's funeral be preached by a selected preacher on a Sunday within a few months after the person had died, during the season when the weather conditions would permit a large audience.

A funeral sermon, more than sixty years ago was preached for the mother of fourteen sons and daughters. After preaching in a sing-song tune for more than an hour, the old preacher closed his sermon with these words:

> "The deceased was a meek Christian, a kind neighbor, a devoted wife, a loving mother and—Lord, what a breeder!"

Men gathered at the country store, spent hours sitting on nail kegs, telling yarns, whittling and throwing knives. They played mumble peg and fox and goose. Most of them wore moustaches, hair that hid their shirt collars, and many wore beards of various length. Many of them chewed tobacco, while few smoked. It was customary for most men to shave only on Saturday evening or Sunday morning.

People enjoyed visiting their neighbors, eating with them and discussing their problems in friendly manner. Few persons who wished to visit other families or take a meal with them awaited an invitation for doing so. Many invitations for a Sunday dinner were accepted at Sunday school or church services. It was customary for many persons, even families, to invite themselves to a neighboring family's home. They knew that they were always welcome. It made little difference when the unexpected guest dropped in at almost mealtime, for extra food might be quickly prepared. Only the Methodist circuit-rider and the church pastors made dinner appointments in advance.

In the long ago, a male sweetheart was a jularker and his sweetheart was a sweetie, darlin' or jusem sweet. There were few automobiles in the rural area during the first decade and a half of the present century, but there were riding horses available to most young men. Still, there was a dearth of sidesaddles, as well as riding habits for females. Often the jularker straddled his horse and the darlin' sat awkwardly behind him, holding to his coat or circling his waist with clasped hands. When there was to be no afternoon rides, the young swain porkskinned his shoes in the absence of shoe polish, crammed a bag of candy into his pocket and faithfully kept his date, arriving at lunch time and declaring, because of bashfulness, that he had already eaten. They sat in the kitchen almost until suppertime, munching crackling bread and discussing the rosy path of life ahead. Unless he had sisters of his own, he did not suspicion that half his sweetie's simulated hair consisted of a cloth rat that helped form her pompadour.

Neighbors seldom borrowed money, but they often borrowed salt, soda, sugar, meal and other commodities, for stores were few and far between and cash was hard to come by. Sometimes a member of a family, going to borrow flour would meet a member of her neighbor's family on her way to borrow coffee from her.

Horse swapping was a delightful custom and business, but commercial horse racing was unknown; rooster fights afforded amusement for most of the population, and shooting matches were held in almost every community.

Exciting debates on numerous disputed subjects were held in the one-room schoolhouses.

Dream books, published and circulated by manufacturers of patent medicines were very popular reading material, especially before breakfast.

In every neighborhood, families visited other families once or twice weekly after the supper dishes were done, gathering to discuss the latest news and gossip, to tell stories and witch tales and play such games as morris and checkers.

Singing conventions and other religious associations brought scores together for miles about. As religious denominational prejudice and strife lessened, interdenominational revival meetings were held.

The fly-specked dried apples and strings of leather-breeches beans, the dried pumpkin looped around small poles nailed to unceiled joists, and the bunches of dried medicinal herbs and roots represented a stock of wealth for many families.

Every country home had its springhouse, where buttermilk, sweet milk and butter were kept cold.

Boys held the family cows while their fathers used a gimlet to bore for hollow horn or to make incisions for hollow tail.

Children took the cat to bed with them for companionship and good luck.

Barefoot boys, going to and from school in the autumn, wore yarn threads around their toes to cure the cracks caused by rain and cold.

Little girls wore their hair in toppies on the tops of their heads and their big sisters and mothers wore theirs most of the time in twists on the back of their heads.

Women wore side combs in their hair and young men wore beauty pins on the lapels of their coats.

The blacksmith's ringing hammer and his sparkling forge attracted every boy and girl in the neighborhood.

The resounding stroke of the woodman's axe rang daily in the forest.

The black gum mallet, the knot maul, the wooden glut and the iron wedge belonged in every tool box.

The music of the old wooden churn kept rhythm with the pulse.

The meal chest guarded its treasure behind every kitchen door.

The horse collar and the ox yoke, the big brass kettle and the wooden applebutter stirrer, the kerosene lamp and the cradle were not found in antique shops or museums.

Almost any evening or early morning would bring the thump, thump of a neighbor householder's hammer as it was used to mend a pair of one of the family member's shoes.

The peddler and his pack never dreamed of the coming of the dime store.

The froe and its riven boards, the drawing knife and the shaving bench were symbols of industry and security.

The best time of the day was when the dinner bell or dinner horn summoned the workers from the fields.

Every family who owned a rocking chair was thought by its neighbors to be on easy street.

The straw and shuck mattress, the mountain-high featherbeds and the baby's cradle, along with the trundlebed, have disappeared.

Even when attending church with her jularker, every young lady had to have a chaperone.

Ah . . . those good old days!

3.
Folklore Trails of the Mountains

THE *long hunters* came first to the mountains of North Carolina. They were the adventurous men who in search of the most valuable fur-bearing animals, spent weeks or months before returning to the lowlands and sometimes they built small cabins in which to live temporarily. An unknown number built more than one cabin, miles apart, maintained a family in each, spent a few weeks or months with one wife while the other spouse or spouses patiently waited in her wild and lonely environment for the hunter's return. Men like Daniel Boone and the Linvilles followed old Indian trails, became acquainted with the region and reported to the people in the old settlements. Other men herded cattle in the mountains during the warm months; botanists, like Michaux and Gray, herborized in much of the area: traders, like Towe, bought furs of the Indians: and explorers, like Bishop Spangenberg, made written descriptions of the region. Between 1725 and 1763 much of the mountain region had become well known.

Men who had found land scarce and competition too fierce in the lowlands of North and South Carolina, Pennsylvania and as far away as New England; the restless, many who objected to the then existing social and economic systems and the landless filtered into the mountains from almost every direction. Many families which had at first intended traveling westwardly until fairly level land was reached decided to settle in the narrow valleys, sheltered coves and upon mountainsides beside or near the trails that crossed the rugged region.

Most of the early settlers had been born in America, but others came from the British Isles. Besides the farm-

A Nineteenth Century Blue Ridge Cabin

ing class, there were cabinet makers and others who had been indentured servants in Massachussetts, Revolutionary War veterans of Pennsylvania, a few who had fled from the witchcraft craze in Salem. All craved land and room enough. They were of the yeoman class as a rule, brave, hardy and self-reliant. There were those of English, Scotch-Irish, German, Dutch and Welsh descent.

From the beginning, a basic agricultural society existed. Food was the first essential. Although most of the land was steep, the soil was rich and the climate permitted the growth of cereal crops and a great variety of vegetables. The expanse of *open* or unfenced lands made the raising of livestock profitable, while chestnuts and acorns assured a bountiful supply of pork. There was game in the forests and the rivers and creeks swarmed with a variety of fish. With patience, anyone might track the wild bee to its hive in a tree, where a bountiful supply of honey was stored.

Corn was the chief crop and every family tilled the acreage needed to supply its wants. The fields were enclosed by fences built of rails split from the chestnut trees, the fences usually containing zigzag panels eight rails high, a stake and a prop. Fences of four to six rails were built to enclose hogs and small animals. Gardens were fenced by sharpened palings. The rail fences did not keep wild turkeys, chipmunks and other rodents from invading the corn fields, beginning when the grain sprouted; consequently, for two or three weeks the farmer's wife and children spent many hours daily marching around the field, shouting and singing.

Many of the very earliest settlers constructed small pole huts for temporary living quarters, often so hurriedly that the bare earth was the floor. The house, having been built during warm weather and hurriedly, a stone furnace was built in the yard for cooking purposes, until colder weather approached. Pieces of bark and large chips of wood sometimes served as dishes. Often the beds were heaps of dry leaves until deerskins, bearskins and wolf skins could be obtained.

Whenever the mountaineer built his permanent home, in most instances, the structure was built with precision-hewed logs, the ends notched carefully to prevent much chinking and daubing. When completed, it was a marvel of strength and craftsmanship. Many first homes contained one or two large rooms under one roof for living and sleeping quarters, while the kitchen and dining space occupied a smaller structure several steps from the main building. This arrangement of detachment enabled the cook from being bothered by the children and visitors when meals were being prepared. Dogs and other pet animals might be more easily kept outside and there was no danger of burning or scalding young children. Later, as prosperity came and the size of the family increased, larger homes, some of them of two stories, were erected, and the kitchen was no longer built in detached fashion from the larger home.

Inasmuch as openings in the log walls had a tendency to weaken the structure, there were few doors and windows. Sometimes the outside doors were built in two sections in order that the upper section might be left open for light and air to enter and smoke to leave, while the lower half remained closed and latched so that small children could not go outside or dogs, pigs and snakes to enter. For many years, the windows had no glass and were furnished with shutters to be opened or closed as the occasion required. On cold or windy days, when the doors were completely closed, candles or brass kerosene lamps furnished all the light that was not given by the blazing wood in the fireplace.

Because the kitchen had formerly occupied a small separate building, the room occupied during most of the day by the family and was larger than the other rooms was called the *big house* or *big room*. Later, it became the *front room,* although it occupied an end of the house, and eventually it became known as the *fire room*. It was the largest of all the rooms and was used as living room—kitchen—dining room. Often it contained a bed, especially when a member of the family was ill.

For many generations, the family's cooking and baking were done in the fireplace. The pots were suspended by pothooks over the blazing logs and bread was baked in an oven covered by hot ashes and coals. For years after the advent of the cookstove, many families refused to use them, sometimes even after one had been installed in the kitchen, as food tasted better, it was said, when prepared in the fireplace.

Most houses were built on hillsides or mountainsides, near springs, for no plumbing was available in those days. Anyway, the best-lying land was used for cultivation. There was another reason: most mountain men liked to feel as near as possible to the mountaintops and the sky and stars. Many felt as did Senator Bob Taylor of Tennessee that "one can stand on the tops of most of the mountains and tickle the feet of the angels." When the house was on a hillside or mountainside, few mountaineers troubled to grade the entire site; consequently, much of the floor was several feet from the ground, resting upon stone foundations or pillars. As he was a great conserver of space, there was an advantage to this, for the space beneath the floor was often used for storage of his tools and equipment and sometimes a place for his hogs to sleep. It also helped in preventing snakes from entering the house in that direction.

Snakes often got inside the houses by crawling through cracks of the puncheon floors and the holes in the daubing between the logs which the bumblebees had made. In early days, before the family retired for the night, the bedding was removed and shaken lest a snake had slithered into the house and was waiting to strike. This practice was called *snaking the beds*.

Most of the tools and equipment which were common until a generation or two ago consisted of grindstones, knot mauls, drawing knives, froes, wooden lasts, wooden vises, wooden flails for threshing grain, bullet moulds, scrapers for hides and pelts, wool cards, spinning wheels, looms and sleds. The sled was one of the most indispensable tools to be found on a farm, and while most of the others have become museum pieces, the sled still occupies a prized position on most farms.

Until a few generations ago, every girl was taught to card wool and tow, dye, weave on the clanging loom, knit stockings and gloves, make her own dyes from roots and barks and to make her own clothing, piece quilts and embroider.

It can be said to the everlasting honor of the pioneers that they built churches almost as soon as they built homes. The first buildings were small log cabins in which religious services were conducted and sermons preached by almost illiterate preachers. The Methodist and Baptist Denominations came first and have dominated the area since.

Public schools, at first supported by the counties and usually taught in a neighborhood church, came late and found that writing schools and *subscription* schools had preceded them a hundred years and more.

The lives of many persons were conditionsd by oral traditions, including good luck and bad luck signs, the meaning of dreams, the signs of the zodiac, the phases of the moon, and those relating to the existenme of ghosts, witches and witch doctors. These various beliefs, for many persons, governed travel, planting and harvesting, nailing on roofs, the deadening of trees, the preparation of foods for winter use, the treatment of disease and the breeding and care of livestock.

Hospitality and friendliness characterized the mountaineer, embracing even the stranger who sought shelter and food in a home which he had seen for the first time. When misfortune came or illness struck, helping hands were extended by neighbors near and far. When houses were to be built, logs rolled in a recently cleared field for planting, a sick man's crop to be tended or harvested, there were house bees, *workings* and neighborly parties. People walked miles to see a new-born baby or to weep at a stranger's funeral. Babies were named for relatives, friends and the *granny womern*.

Families visited one another often, discussed the weather, exchanged news and gossip and enjoyed the best meals families could prepare.

It was once an insult to refuse hospitality, even though it might mean eating an extra meal. *Lunch* was not in the vocabulary of the mountaineer, for the food he served was meant *to stick to one's ribs*.

The justice of the peace ranked socially with the

preacher, for he judged the people in their petty disputes, wrote their legal papers and joined their sons and daughters in marriage. He varied his marriage ceremony to suit the occasion, the shortest one on record being: "Stand, jine hands, hitched."

Work and recreation were mixed at corn shuckings, log rollings, apple peelings, bean stringings, molasses boilings, hog killings, quiltings and other *workings*. All these were festive occasions; when laughter and good humor, lightened the tasks, feasts were prepared, and hours of fun, banjo music and Old Virginia Reel followed the finished tasks.

Shooting matches, wrestling contests, rooster fights, various kinds of parties, square dances, string music concerts, singings, neighborhood parties with dinner on the grounds, serenades for the newly married, snake hunting parties, sapping parties and nut hunting were enjoyable social customs throughout the mountains. The folkways also included setting dumb suppers, playing both indoor and outdoor games . . . the telling of witch tales and ghost stories, and fortune telling by palmistry and coffeee grounds in cups. Even a death was followed by a festive wake in the home of the deceased before the coming of undertaking establishments.

Only a few holidays were celebrated and these included Thanksgiving Day, Christmas, New Year's Day and Easter.

Old Christmas was a special day in many homes, as oral traditions held sway, especially after the supper table was cleared.

For many decades and until stores became plentiful, the children's Christmas toys and gifts were mainly homemade. There were dolls, yarn balls, whistles, geehaw whimmydiddles or ziggerboos, rattle traps, noisemakers or bull roars and flipperdingers. Besides toys, there were cakes of maple sugar, items of clothing and multi-colored home-knitted mittens and stockings. Husband and wife exchanged gifts of clothing and handmade gifts.

4.
In the Old Days

MOTHERS made all their children's clothes, knit their stockings and gloves.

Stores carried lanterns, horse shoes, ox shoes and buggy whips, and had hitching rails conveniently located outside.

Almost every boy and young man had either a French harp or a Jews harp.

Mothers made all their children's clothes, knit the family's stockings and gloves.

They bartered their homegrown products for commodities which the stores sold.

Young men and girls went on hayrides in the moonlight.

Those who didn't burn kerosene lamps made their own candles.

Men made their own axe handles, mended the family's shoes, bottomed their chairs with hickory splints and split rails for their fences.

Much of their furniture was handmade, the mattresses were of straw and nearly every family picked its ducks and geese and made pillows and featherbeds of the feathers.

Young women curled their hair with hot iron curlers or wore it in pompadours, with cloth *rats* hidden underneath and pasted little spit curls on their foreheads.

They helped one another shuck their corn, string their beans, peel their apples for drying or applebutter and make their molasses. The men helped one another roll and pile the logs of a *newground* while the women-folk quilted new-pieced quilts and helped prepare the sumptous feast for the noon meal.

Women picked burrs from the wool, washed, carded and spun it into yarn for knitting or weaving.

Folk usually went to bed with the hens and arose with the roosters.

Every family kept at least one rooster for announcing the time of morning and getting up time.

When the supply of matches had become exhausted, a member of the family hurried to a neighbor's home to borrow fire.

Box suppers, cake walks, debates in the schoolhouse, square dances, string music and parties were enjoyable events.

Most men wore boots and women wore high button shoes.

A buggy ride was the next most enjoyable event to the experience of riding in a surrey with a fringe on the edge of its top.

Beef and turkey shoots and rooster fights were great recreational events.

Every man and boy carried a Barlowe knife for general purposes.

Candidates for county offices, on speaking dates in the schoolhouses, proved great attractions for almost everyone.

Hog-killing time was a holiday for a family and its neighbors.

Those who engaged in fox hunts were never happier than when listening to "the heavenly music of their hounds a-giving tongue out thar."

Young women delighted themselves and others and released much pent-up emotion by singing *Fair Margaret And Sweet William* and other old love ballads.

Men rived their own boards for their roofs, fashioned their locust fence posts, did their cobbling, repaired their hoes and other tools and plowed their fields by horse and ox power.

During a severe thunderstorm, the safest place from lightning was in a darkened room or under a featherbed.

On days when the weather was inclement, men crowd-

Eagle Hotel, Asheville, 1875.

ed the country stores, sat on nail kegs and played morris, fox and goose or checkers, whittled on pieces of soft wood, swapped jokes and gossip and discussed the latest news.

There were plenty of fish in the creeks and rivers and game in the woodlands to be had when chores on the farm were not pressing.

Corn to be ground into meal at the water-powered grist mill was carried in strong white bags on the shoulder.

Women did their weekly wash at the *wash place,* using a large iron pot, a battle block and a battle paddle and homemade soap.

Soap was made from grease and lye. The lye had been manufactured by allowing water to run through wood ashes in an ash hopper in the yard.

Girls had their ears pierced with needles, put threads through the holes until they healed, then inserted flashy earrings.

Beauty pins were popular with both young men and women.

Women wore celluloid side combs and a large back comb in their hair, used hatpins for holding their small-crowned hats on their head.

Most men had their hair cut by a neighbor, but those who had a barber to do it paid twenty-five cents.

Most cigarette smokers rolled their own from Stud smoking tobacco.

Women's skirts were ankle-length and girls wore skirts that reached midway between knees and ankles.

The best spring tonic for purifying the blood was a dose of molasses and sulphur.

Unless the weather was extremely rainy or cold, a large crowd always met the afternoon mail at the post office.

The well-attended singing conventions, church associations and country fairs were made possible by persons riding either horseback or in wagons.

Children wore little bags of asafetida on strings around their necks to ward off diphtheria.

Barefoot boys with cracks under their toes wore yarn threads in the cracks to heal them and stonebruises were cured by a bandage of fat bacon.

The katydid's rasping tones indicated that frost was only six weeks away.

Shuck beans, crackling bread, cream butter and sourwood honey provided a meal fit for any mountaineer or king.

A cradle for the baby was necessary in order that the mother might perform her multitudinous tasks.

Boys until teen-age wore knee pants and waists with long flowing collars.

Sunday school excursions were run by passenger trains to nearby towns and cities.

Five dollars would buy a wheelbarrowful of groceries.

Motels and restaurants did not prevent mountaineers from displaying their innate hospitality to friend and traveler alike.

The old days and the old ways are memories of the past.

5.
The Wake

THE Wake was originated by the Irish, but it came into full flower in the mountains of North Carolina many decades before the coming of the undertaking establishments. The Wake was intended to be a gathering of sympathetic relatives and friends in the home of the deceased, for paying respect to the dead and to dispel partially the gloom and loneliness that had settled upon the members of the family, but it came about that the all-night vigil demanded a degree of amusement and restrained gaiety. As time passed, it often became, after a preliminary time of solemnity, a period of song, laughter, games, gossip, courtship and what-not.

When it had become apparent that Old Man Jordan was near the end of life's trail, that mid-afternoon, visiting relatives moved the bed on which he lay from its accustomed place against the wall to the center of the floor in order, it was thought, that the traditional invisible death-watch angels might take their places: one at yan corner of the bed, one at its furder corner, one at this here corner and the fourth at that thar corner. The fifth death-watch angel, as invisible as the others, was believed to be standing near the open door, awaiting the arrival of the riderless horse and wagon that would come noiselessly, quite unseen, to bear away the released spirit of Old Man Jordan and leave it beyond the mythical River of Jordan.

Aunt Viddie, the sick man's wife, stood beside the bed, slowly waving a brush of green-leaved twigs in an effort to frighten the houseflies that buzzed above the patient's face. For several minutes, the swish of the flybrush was the only audible sound, as the three men sat with heads bowed and eyes closed, then she gently laid the fly-brush upon the bed and turned to the men present.

"He's gone," she announced in sorrowful tones. "My old man jest shut his eyes peaceful-like and kicked the bucket."

The men suddenly started, despite the happening of the expected.

"Is he dead?" one of them asked.

"He is as dead as a door nail," she affirmed, not intending to be irreverent. Turning to the man to whom she had spoken, she said: "Move the hives and tell the bees that their master is dead."

The superstitious belief that, unless the bees were told of the death of the head of the family, they would leave had been brought into the mountains by a Pioneer ancestor from New England generations before.

As silently and as ghost-like as a modern undertaker, the man tiptoed from the room.

Outside, from force of habit, he paused for a moment, half-expecting to see the phantom horse and wagon, but there was no shimmering, no faint resemblance, and he moved on quickly. He walked to the backyard, where the four hives of bees stood spectral-like in the evening shadows. Slowly and carefully he moved each hive a quarter-inch, stooped and whispered, "The master is dead."

Aunt Viddie discussed the making of the casket by the neighborhood coffin-makers; the spot in the family graveyard where the grave would be dug and the preacher-man who would funeralize the corpse.

While community cemeteries were becoming common in the countryside, many families maintained their private burial grounds on their farms, mainly for the reason as expressed by one aged man: "Should hants come snooping around, we'll know that they are former members of the family, and we'll not be scairt." For three generations, there had been a family graveyard on the farm which Old Man Jordan had inherited, and there is where he was to be buried.

Often there were exacting restrictions relative to the burial of relatives in these small cemeteries. The plots had invisible dividing lines which were to prevent the good from being placed near even a close relative who had been judged as having strayed too far outside the straight and narrow path of rectitude. Too, on the First Resurrection, all the graves in the preferred area should be found open—no some gone—some left fashion.

"Be sure," said *Aunt* Viddie, "not to bury my old man anear his pap. I remember the countless times Jordan's mother set her old man's bed on the front porch of their home in order to let her neighbors know there had been a split-up between them because he had tried to take the bridle bits out of his mouth by jawing her and refusing to obey her orders. Sometimes his bed sat on the porch a week or more, while the passing neighbors laughed, before he would come sneaking home and apologize for his objections to her wanting to do his thinking for him."

After the necessary instructions had been given, she seated herself in the rocking chair.

"I knowed for months that one of us would leave this world afore the year ended," she said. "The first corn silk I seed last spring was white. Several times our old rooster hopped into the door, stuck his head outside and crowed, which was an omen that one of us would be leaving before the year ended. The death-watch beetles clicked in the walls and in our old furniture terrible. A month ago I seed a falling star."

The man who had moved the bees and taken the correct measurements prepared to leave for the coffin shop.

"I'll norrate the news as best I can that Old Man Jordan is dead," he obliged.

"We'll have a setting-up tonight," she told him.

"I'll norrate that, too," he assured her.

She arose from the creaky rocking chair and announced that she was retiring for the night. At the bedroom

The Wake: a pause when the coffin came in.

door she paused and turned to the men sitting nearby.

"Before saying good night," she told them, "I'll give you a few warnings which, maybe, you don't know.

"Don't wash a person's clothes on New Year's Day. If you do or have it done, you will wash that person's corpse before the end of the year.

"If you sweep trash from the floor to the outside of the house, instead of into the fireplace, between Christmas and New Year's Day, there will be a death in the family before twelve months have passed.

"If you have an Old Christmas flower planted in your dooryard, you know that it will break through the ground on Old Christmas Morning. If you fail to make a wish while looking at it on the day it appears, your cattle will be on their knees praying for you come next Old Christmas midnight.

"If you take ashes from the fireplace between Christmas and New Year's Day, there will be a death in the family before the end of the coming year."

Soon after nightfall, several persons brought prepared food and, as the attendance increased, women began baking and cooking additional foods. Green coffee beans were parched in a skillet, ground in a handmill held between the knees; then brewed in a large iron pot above the fireplace coals.

As the evening wore on, the Wake became more festive. Jokes were told and riddles propounded, then came a round of tongue twisters. A young lady sang *Black Jack Davis* and *Barbara Allen,* a young man played the banjo which he had brought along, while an elderly man cut the pigeon wing. Two men started the game of morris and two other men tried their hands at Fox And Goose. The young lady who had done the singing and her boyfriend went outside and courted in the moonlight on the farther end of the porch. Inside the kitchen young ladies had their fortunes told from the formation of coffee grounds in twirled cups. As the night progressed, the hungry ate and drank coffee at intervals,

Stage Arrives at Warm Spring Hotel, 1875.

a jug of whiskey was repeatedly passed to those who craved a drink of moonshine.

The coffin-makers had hurried their job and, shortly after midnight, they came around a corner of the house and shoved the coffin onto the end of the porch. The courting couple saw the ghastly object in the moonlight, imagined ghosts had brought it, gave two piercing screams and fainted. Several minutes were required to revive and calm them.

For a while after the casket containing the body was placed upon chairs in the family room, a solemn quietness held sway, then someone risked a witty remark and the festive spirit flamed again. The two men who had spent most of the night playing Fox And Goose placed a small tin kerosene lamp on the casket and, one standing on either side of it, resumed their game until the day was dawning.

As each person ended the night of celebrating the Wake, a pinch of earth was obtained in the dooryard and sprinkled upon the casket, with the doleful words, "Ashes to ashes and dust to dust."

6.
The Lineback Ghost

DURING the declining days of the Confederacy, an old Irish peddler, physically unfit for military duty, operated in the Linville River and North Toe River Valleys. He was a hunchback, with very large blood-shot eyes, protruding upper teeth and unusually large hands, all of which caused him to present a somewhat frightful appearance. He carried his heavy black pack of assorted small wares upon his shoulders, peddled his merchandise from house to house in the sparsely settled area and accepted Confederate currency in his transactions. Some of his items were bartered for bed and board in the log cabins that proved hospitable to him.

His irregular circuits, made on foot, led him over narrow roads and blazed trails, through mostly wooded areas and rhododendron thickets, across ridges and mountains and into yawning hollows and narrow valleys. His walking cane was long and heavy, made of hickory and used sometimes for warding off vicious dogs.

As the war drew to a close and the legal tender of the Confederacy depreciated in value, his pockets often bulged with rolls of bills that, to many persons, appeared to be fabulous sums.

Whenever darkness overtook him, he spent the night, if the home admitted him, entertaining the family and any guests who happened to be present with his rich folklore. Well-liked as he was, there were those whose greedy eyes often dwelt in covetousness upon his pocketsful of almost worthless money, which he was fond of displaying.

Finally, the peddler made his rounds no more. For sometime, it was believed that either he had decided on more lucrative areas or had returned permanently to his home in Lenoir, but finally his empty pack was found beside a hurriedly heaped grave under a large oak tree that grew upon a spur of the Blue Ridge, between the headwaters of Squirrel Creek and the present town of Crossnore.

Shortly after the war ended, a man by the name of John Lineback moved into the area and built himself a small store of whipsawed lumber and puncheons within a hundred yards of the unmarked grave under the oak tree. The main room of the building was for the merchandise, while a lean-to, attached to the rear of the building served as his sleeping quarters, as theft and burglary were common in those days, the merchant wished to occupy the building at night as a deterrent to robbery.

After the building was completed and the merchandise stocked, the merchant told his customers that the ghost of the peddler had helped him erect the building by nailing a board as often as he himself had placed one.

The ghost, he said, was visible, had huge flaming eyes and protruding teeth that resembled pumpkin seeds. It had never spoken, but sometimes uttered a horrible cackling laugh, especially when it had placed a board more quickly than had the merchant. What was more, when the storekeeper retired for the night in the little lean-to, the specter entered the locked store and hurried back and forth across the floors and behind the counters, rattled the tinware and dropped green coffee beans beside the scales. The merchant was unsure, he said, as to whether the ghost was taking inventory of his stock or trading with other ghosts. The money in the cash register was always the same at morning as it had been at close of business on the previous evening. On several instances, the ghost had crept to his bedside, jerked off the covers, blew out the flame of the sputtering candle, then became quiet until another night. Perhaps, he added, it had returned to its grave under the oak tree on the hill.

Most persons were horrified by Lineback's weird story, and it came about that many late travelers at night, either afoot or on horseback, avoided passing very near the store by making a circuitous new trail through the woods some distance away.

Because some persons, less superstitious than many others, expressed doubt regarding the ghost, the merchant offered a reward of five dollars to the man who would spend a night alone in the lean-to. For a long while, no one accepted the offer of the reward.

As the story of the ghost and the news of the offered reward spread, they eventually reached the ears of Philo Pritchard of Watauga County.

Late one afternoon, Pritchard appeared and announced that he had come to claim the reward. He was known to be a member of a courageous family. His sister had been a Confederate soldier until her true sex was discovered and her husband had fought in both the Confederate and Union Armies. At dusk, the merchant locked the outside doors, gave Pritchard the keys and told him that the reward and a good breakfast would be awaiting him at daylight.

"The candle in the lean-to is burned down," Linebeck told him. "Better walk with me to the house for another."

At thick dusk, as Pritchard retraced his steps in the light of the full moon, the merchant saw him buckle his pistol holster more tightly, unlock the door of the lean-to and go inside.

Pritchard closed and locked the door, lit the candle and placed it on the small table beside the bed. Within a few minutes he disrobed and retired.

Seemingly, he was not frightened, but he found sleep a difficult thing. Once or twice he raised himself upon an elbow and looked toward the table to see that the pistol still lay within his reach, then he lay on his side, facing the flickering candle.

Suddenly the ghost, carrying a little lighted tin lamp, entered the room and stood grinning beside him, its eyes gleaming like coals of fire and its protruding teeth resembling pumpkin seeds. For a moment it stood beside the bed, then jerking the covers from the bed, said in true Irish brogue:

"Begorra! There are two of us here."

"Y-y-e-s," answered the thoroughly excited Pritchard, "but if you will be so kind as to allow me to put on my britches, there won't be but one of us here."

Pritchard's clothes were soon donned and, his teeth clicking liked a scared screech owl's bills, he, never thinking of his pistol, unlocked, flung open the door and dashed as fast as his feet could carry him down the narrow moonlit road.

After running for a mile, he sat down, gasping for breath; then he looked up, and there stood the ghost.

"We've had a pretty good race," said the ghost.

"We certainly have," Pritchard panted; "and if you will give me time to get back my breath, we'll have another good one."   —Told by Artie G. Laws.

7.
The Ghosts of Whispering Creek

IN 1864, Pretty Polly lived with her invalid mother in a little log cabin on the banks of Whispering Creek, while her father fought as a Union soldier somewhere in Virginia. Because her eyes were as blue as the sky, her hair a flaming red and her form as willowy as that of a mountain nymph, all who knew her declared she was the most beautiful young woman in all the valley. One day each week, she did the family wash, battling it on a block near the creek bank until her laundry was the cleanest and whitest in all the valley.

During the Civil War, public sentiment in Whispering Creek Valley, as it was in most communities of Western North Carolina, was fiercely divided concerning the struggle. Pretty Polly's father was fighting with the Federals and her mother had forbidden her even to be on speaking terms with the Confederate soldiers, who sometimes passed the road that crossed the creek near her battling block. As a dutiful and obedient daughter, Pretty Polly made it a habit to ignore the wavings and greethings of the few soldiers in gray who chanced to pass her place.

Came the day when a dashing young Confederate soldier, booted and spurred, with a sword at his side, and riding a big black stallion, reined his thirsty horse for a drink from the sparkling waters near her big black pot and battling block. There was something different about the handsome young soldier, Polly thought, as her pleased eyes swept over him, and she unthoughtedly violated her mother's mandate. Before the conversation ended, she invited him "to light and rest a spell." while she brought him some cold sweet milk from the springhouse and a piece of freshly baked gingerbread. Before departing, he informed her that he was Captain of a Home Guard company in an adjoining county.

Only two or three times did he pass that way again, but tongues began to wag that Pretty Polly had been seen in the arms of a man in gray and eventually a rumor to the effect that Pretty Polly had told a close friend that she was madly in love with the handsome soldier reached her mother's ears. The sum total of it all was that, under the mother's strict orders, Pretty Polly told her lover that she could not see him again.

Pretty Polly's father died valiantly at Cold Harbor and the handsome Confederate captain perished when Stoneman's Raid swept through Western North Carolina.

The little log cabin is gone from the banks of Whispering Creek; Pretty Polly's big black pot, smelling of homemade lye soap, her battling block and battling stick have long since vanished; and she of the laughing blue eyes and the flaming red hair lies on the little knoll above the cabin site, with only a creek rock for her headstone. But the folk of this quaint little valley today, each generation told by the one before it, well know that she yet sometimes meets her handsome Rebel soldier, as she did in the summer of 1864.

On nights when there is no moon, the courageous who goes alone can see a light rising slowly from her grave; then moving more rapidly above the ground, as a woman with a lantern would run to meet her lover, until it reaches the bank of Whispering Creek, where another and brighter light is waiting. Then, for a moment only, as the lovers meet, there is a vision of long red hair against a gray coat, before the lights vanish in the mountain mists.

8.
The Ghosts of Yellow Mountain Gap

YELLOW Mountain Gap, lying between the Big Yellow and the Roan Mountains, was the highest point of the old Yellow Mountain Road which ran from the eastern foothills of the Yellow Mountains into the Watauga Settlements. It followed Bright's Trace, which in turn followed an old Indian Trail unknown hundreds of years old. In earliest days of settlement and for many decades thereafter, it was the only road available for travel between the Yadkin and Catawba River Valleys to the lands west of the mountains. As the population in what are now Tennessee and Kentucky grew, it became a trunk highway for wagons and for driving droves of cattle, mules and turkeys to the seaboard markets. The Over the Mountain Men and their horses, more than twelve hundred strong, traveled it from Sycamore Shoals to

Quaker Meadows and thence to help crush Colonel Ferguson's army at King's Mountain.

In the early days, pioneers of the North Carolina mountains lived miles from one another and wherever the scattered settlers built their homes and cleared fields, their places of abode were called *clearings, choppings* or *Places.*

Sam Bright of Salisbury entered a large tract of land on which he built a great log house, barns and outbuildings near the trace that bore his name and his settlement became known at Bright's Place. Although he was a rough, lawless man, he was hospitable and generous to those who passed or sought refuge from storms and cold. None was stranger long.

One year saw winter begin earlier than usual in the mountains. A sudden severe cold spell toward the end of October caused two large families and a man and his wife, remembered only as Jonathan and Matilda, to seek shelter at Bright's Place. For more than a week the intense cold prevailed, then suddenly the weather improved appreciably and Jonathan and Matilda, against the advice of others, decided to resume walking to their journey's end somewhere in the Watauga Settlements.

As they disappeared up the old Yellow Mountain Road, Jonathan carried a bundle of what appeared to be clothing on the end of a short pole, and Matilda, with a deerskin bag which she had said contained the money received for the sale of their home near Salisbury.

While the couple was still in sight, Bright shook his head and muttered, "They're risking the mountain weather too much. It's thirty miles to the Shelving Rock, and not a house between here and there!"

Before Jonathan and Matilda had tramped half the distance to Yellow Mountain Gap, the temperature began falling, and, halfway up the narrow Roaring Creek Valley, the wind, sweeping into their faces and howling like a pack of wolves over the ridges and through the coves, almost froze to the marrow.

The temperature continued falling. It became so cold that the wildcats did not scream and the wolves were huddled in their lairs on the side of Roan Mountain. Nothing alive moved in the laurel slicks of the sides of Yellow Mountain Gap.

The extreme cold lasted only a few days, the winds became silent and the sun shone through the clouds, warming the late October air. The two families left behind at Bright's Place, having resumed their journey, went aside to water their horses at the nearby Big Elk Spring, a few hundred yards below Yellow Mountain Gap and were startled to find the frozen bodies of Jonathan and Matilda in its waters, where they had sought refuge from the freezing air.

The old Yellow Mountain Road fell into disuse many decades later, when the population had greatly increased and a better and miles-saving road, now known as 19E, was constructed. Only tourists, hunters and persons searching for strayed livestock wander over the old roadbed to Yellow Mountain Gap today.

When the harvest moon is bright, fox hunters at night on the sides of the Big Yellow and Roan Mountains sometimes pause in silence as they listen to Jonathan's ghost, calling from Yellow Mountain Gap in hollow tones, like the winds that sweep over the mountains:

"Matilda! Oh, Matilda, Matilda!"

And another voice like that of a woman's, but more like the shriek of a wildcat, answers in half-glad, half-sad tones, which quiver and echo over the ridges and in the coves:

"Jonathan! Oh, Jonathan!"

9.
Tongue Twisters

BLACK bug's blood.
Shave a cedar shingle thin.
Don't you think the lasts last well?
Simple Sister Susan sits in the soup.
The sixth sheik's sixth sheep is sick.
Is this, then, the team that Thomas tried?
Ten times ten and ten times ten and ten times ten again.
Sam sawed six or seven slim slick sycamore saplings.
Little Tiny Toes had ten tiny little toes.
She sells sea shells. Does she still sell sea shells? Sea shells she sells.

Susan shines shoes and socks. Does Susan shine shoes and socks? Where are the shoes and socks that Susan shines?

Slender Sam Slimber, sleek and slim, sawed six slender saplings.

Funny Fanny Flynn fried five fat fish for five frightened fishermen.

A pied piper blew a penny pipe for a penny pieman and a penny pieman gave a penny pie for the pied piper's penny pie.

Sam Slick's sloppy shoes and socks shocked Susan at the shoe shop.

Let ten little men in ten seconds ten find out by their own brain.

Theophilus Thistle, the successful thistle-sifter, in sifting a sieve of unsifted thistles, thrust three thousand thistles through the thick of his thumb.

  Susan Botter bought some butter,
  "But," she said, "this butter's bitter;
  If I put it in my batter,

A Regular Menagerie, 1875

It will make my batter bitter;
But a bit of better butter
Will but make by batter better."
So she bought a bit of butter,
Better than the bitter butter,
Made her bitter batter better.
So it was better Betty Botter
Bought a bit of better butter.

Lawrence, the rogue, lengthened the rope of Pat's pig in a poke.

Twine three twines thrice three times.

Peter Parker picked a peck of pickled peppers. If Peter Parker picked a peck of pickled peppers, where is the peck of pickled peppers Peter Parker picked?

Sam seined six slim slick sickly snakes.

The sea seetheth and ceaseth not seething.

He thrust his fists into the mists and still insists he sees the ghosts.

The seething sea ceaseth and thus the seething sea sufficieth us.

Sue sighted six slim shapely slick saplings.

10.
Riddles

A HILLFULL a hole full, but you can't catch a bowlful.
Ans.: Smoke.

What is it that goes all over the house during the day and stands in the corner at night? Ans.: The broom.

It can run and can't walk;
It has a tongue and can't talk. Ans.: A wagon.

A woman said to her son,
"Thy father is my father,
And thy grandfather my husband;
Thou are my son, and I am thy sister." Ans.: Lot's daughter talking to her son.

It's white and black and read all over. Ans.: A newspaper.

The more you feed it
The more it will grow high,
But if you give it water,
Then it will die. Ans.: A fire.

From house to house it goes,
So sure and yet so slight;
And whether it rains or whether it snows,
It sleeps outside all night. Ans.: A path.

Thirty white horses on a red hill,
Now they clamp, now they stamp,
And now they stand still. Ans.: Your teeth.

Brothers and sisters have I none,
But this man's father is my father's son. Ans. The man was the speaker's son.

Who died before his mother was born? Ans.: Abel. Eve was not born.

The oldest man who ever lived died before his father. Explain. Ans.: Methusaleh's father, Enoch, was translated.

There was a man of Adam's race
Who had a certain dwelling place.
'Twas not in heaven, 'twas not in hell
Nor on the earth the man did dwell;
'Twas not composed of human art,
Brick, stone or wood had any part.
If you know this man of fame,
Tell where he lived and what his name. Ans.: Jonah in the whale's belly.

There was a little green house,
And in the little green house,
There was a little brown house,
And in the little brown house,
There was a little white house,
And in the little white house
there was a little heart. Ans.: A chestnut.

What flies forever
And rests never? Ans.: The wind.

What has legs and doesn't walk, face and doesn't talk? Ans.: A clock.

Round the house and round the house
And there lies a white glove at the window. Ans.: Snow.

11.
Those Seasons Long Ago

SPRING

CLIMATICALLY, the seasons in the mountains long ago were about the same as today, but they were for other things.

Spring was for sowing a lettuce bed under its canvas cover.

For rolling the logs into heaps in the *newground* and burning them for early spring planting of the virgin soil.

For harrowing the fields with wooden harrows of locust teeth drawn by a yoke of oxen.

For the peddler and his pack of small wares.

For scouring the floors of the home with a hickory scrub broom and white sand.

For repairing and building rail fences, with a locust post in each corner.

For turning the stock loose to range the unfenced acreage of the mountains.

For the entire family's working from sunup to sundown, planting and hoeing farm crops on the steep and rocky mountainside.

The time for fishing for the trout and hornyhead in rivers and creeks.

For women and girls to gather twigs of birch, mahogany and sweet gum for toothbrushes.

For boys to make whistles from buckeye bark and popguns and squirt guns from elder stalks.

For children to discard their footwear and go barefoot until the frost came again.

For whole families and groups of families to form sapping parties for obtaining and eating the delicious sap of birch, mahogany and chestnut.

For dosing the family with sassafras tea or molasses and sulphur as blood tonics.

For enjoying the aromatic tea of the spicewood.

For children to hunt birds' nests and men to shoot hawks and woodchucks.

SUMMER

Summer for whole families to hoe in the gardens and fields every week that contained a Friday.

For adults and children to splash in the old swimming hole on Saturday afternoons.

For camp meetings, religious Associations and Sunday School Conventions.

For homecoming dinners on the church grounds.

For picking and canning blackberries.

For beanstringings, candy pullings and dinners of secret societies.

For making jellies, pickles and jams.

For taking Sunday picnics on the tops of mountains.

For gathering crude drugs for home remedies and to barter at the stores, when the soil was too wet to cultivate crops.

For picking the geese and ducks and shearing the sheep which had been missed during the spring search.

For taking hayrides on moonlit nights.

For preparing exhibitions to be shown at the county fair.

For Sunday School train excursions.

AUTUMN

Autumn was for gathering and storing the bountiful yield of field, orchard and forest.

For hog-killing, making sausage and preparing cracklings for delicious crackling cornbread.

For corn shuckings, molasses boilings and quilting parties.

For herding and driving the cattle from the mountain ranges.

For gathering and storing chestnuts, walnuts, butternuts and hickory nuts for winter use, and for gathering the late apples for winter storage.

For threshing the wheat and rye and making new straw mattresses.

For debates, box suppers, song fests and square dances.

For singing schools and writing schools.

For school entertainments, magic shows and hand-cranked moving picture shows.

For various *Togethers* and other celebrations.

For the time that life was not socially dull or drab.

WINTER

For women to piece and embroider quilts, card and spin wool, knit stockings and mittens and pulse warmers.

For young ladies who wished to add to their hope chests by tatting, forming a pretty garment or making a coverlid.

For square dances, fiddle and banjo music, church revival meetings, neighborhood sings, home parties and story-telling hours.

For trapping the fur-bearing animals and stretching them upon boards for curing, for making and eating fried apple pies, taking corn to the water-powered grist mill a mile or more distant between freezing spells of weather, caring for the new-born lambs, wading snowdrifts to feed the stock and milk the cows.

For feeding the wandering preachers chicken and ham and letting them sleep on mountain-high beds.

For the reading of Scripture, asking and answering folk Bible questions and telling children Bible stories of such characters as Noah, Daniel and Goliath.

For thankfulness at evening time for peace and comfort and plenty and a home, however humble, usually debt-free and unmortgaged.

12.
Folk Bible Questions

WHEN was a rooster's crow heard by every living human being on earth? Ans.: In Noah's ark. Gen. 7:13-23.

Who was the most ambitious man? Ans.: Jonah. Even a whale couldn't keep him down.

Is the Book of Hesekiah in the Old Testament or the New Testament? Ans.: It is not in the Bible.

What time of day was it when Adam was created? Ans.: Just before Eve.

What did Adam and Eve do when they were forced out of Eden? Ans.: They raised Cain. Gen. 3:23; 4:1.

Why did not Moses take any bees into the ark? Ans.: It was Noah who took the living creatures into the ark.

Why did not the lions eat Daniel? Ans.: He was too full of grit.

Who took meat with him when embarking on a long voyage? Ans.: Noah. He took Ham into the ark. Gen. 7:13.

What was Adam's longest day? Ans.: The first. It had no Eve. Gen. 2:18.

Who was the wickedest man of the Bible? Ans. Moses, because he broke all the Commandments at once.

Why was Saint Paul like a horse? Ans.: He liked Timothy. Timothy 2:1-2.

Who was the hungriest man of the Bible? Ans.: Noah, because he went 150 days without finding Arat. Airy (e'er a) rat. Gen. 8:3-4.

13.
Children's Games and Pastime

MANY children's games that were brought into the mountains in early days and were played for generations are still popular today, while others cannot be recognized because of their variations. For lack of simplicity or other reasons, many proved unpopular and were forgotten.

Hopscotch, known first in the American Colonies as *scotch-hoppers*, was practiced many centuries ago by the Greek and Spartan women.

There have been many variations of *tag* and the game is sometimes called *Glove*. The players form a circle and hold hands and one player walks around the circle, gently taps another player and attempts to take the tagged one's place.

Cats-cradle or *crow's nest* was played by a long string or piece of twine being looped over the extended fingers of both hands in symmetrical pattern, then a second player was required to remove the twine without losing the loops, then fashioning another different pattern.

Single or double bats was played with balls and bats by the *ins* while other players in the field attempted to catch the ball and succeed as batter.

The game of *bull pen* was played by any number of children, four of whom occupied bases forming a square, the others in the pen. After the ball was passed several times to allow it to become *hot* a player tried to hit one in the pen. Failing to do so, the unhit player took the thrower's base. In case of a hit, the four basemen ran and the struck person attempted to hit anyone of the runners with the ball. Succeeding in doing so, he took a corner base. At times, the basemen would *juggle* by leaving their bases, getting into a huddle, while one of them hid the ball under his coat. Returning to their bases, they awaited those inside the pen to come within striking distance of the secret ball holder.

Leap frog was a popular game for most boys.

Hide and whoop was played wherever shrubs or other objects afforded a hiding place. The hunter tried to find the hidden players, one by one, then return to the home base without being caught by the found one.

Bird in the cage was played by four children forming a cage by clasping hands of upraised arms. Two or three cages were formed and the bird changed cages while the cat attempted to catch it.

Rope-jumping, usually while reciting rhymes, was a favorite.

Kitty Wants A Corner: All the players took corners and the kitty passed by each, saying "Kitty wants a corner." The players were required to change corners often, when Kitty attempted to obtain a vacant one. The player losing became the kitty.

Especially when the now antique large agate marbles were plentiful, most boys found the game very popular.

Jack in the Bush and *Even and Odd* were played as guessing games before chestnuts became extinct.

Honey Pot was played by a number of children squatting upon the ground or floor, with clasping hands underneath their legs, while two others attempted to carry them. *Rotten Eggs* was played almost identical, except the two players held the *egg* by their arms and shook them soundly. Those whose hands unclasped were rotten eggs.

Fox and dogs was played where there were bushes and shrubs, usually by larger boys. The fox attempted to elude the dogs by running, hiding and reaching logs or large rocks as safe spots or dens.

Witch and Chicks was played by any number of children, the largest child being the Old Hen, the next largest being the Old Witch. The chicks clasped arms around one another and formed a line behind Old Hen, while the Old Witch stood in front. Old Hen started the game by repeating: "Craney, craney, craney, oh, I went to the spring to wash my big toe and when I got back one of my blackeyed chicks was gone. Cluck, Old Witch, do you have it?" Old Witch answers, "Yes, and I intend to have another," whereupon she dives for the last chick in the line, which is continuously maneuvered in an attempt to make the chick-catching as difficult as possible. When the last chick is caught, the game is renewed. Ante-over is a familiar and popular game today.

Top spinning and kite flying were popular pastime for many boys for decades.

The old game of stop and go is known today as red light.

All the Birds of the Air later became Pretty Bird. In the old game, each player assumed the name of a well-known bird and the odd player became the slave, with the name of the less-known bird. The player that guessed his name became the slave or leader.

Blind Man's Bluff was either an outdoor or indoor game and when the blindfolded player neared an obstacle, Blacksnake was called as a warning.

Hot or Cold for many generations was a popular inside game which was played by a number of children attempting to find a hidden object.

William Trim a Toe, Thimble (in which penalties were levied, Slap Out and Club Fist were popular games in the olden days.

Betty Bows, large cloth dolls, were once very amusing to those in the know-how, but ofen frightening to the uninitiated boy or girl. The Betty Bow was held in front of a bed coverlet or quilt by someone hidden underneath the bed. When everything was ready, the children were taken into a dimly lit room and seated for the performance. Upon being talked to by the leader or someone in the know-how, the Betty Bow answered questions by nodding its head, danced and cavorted, always obeying orders. When tension was high, the Betty Bow was suddenly tossed toward the unitiated child or children who usually shrieked loudly.

14.
Weather Wisdom

SINCE antiquity, men have been interested in weather and what causes it. Perhaps the ancient shepherds, who were more watchful than ordinary men, were the first to look for signs that would indicate the morrow's weather. Farmers, who lived near nature and who depended upon weather for success or failure, were observant of moon, clouds and winds. Most civilized nations came to have men who spent most of their time exploring the secrets of nature, and England was no exception. Sir Humphrey Davy, a very careful observer, studied natural phenomena, gathered material which pertained to the prediction of weather and explained the most reasonable *weather omens* which had been derived from popular observation. When men came to America from the British Isles, they brought their *weather omens* with them and they and their descendants modified or dropped some of them and added others which close observation made them believe fitted the geographical region.

Signs from animals, birds, insects, worms and snakes, they believed, as well as those from sun, moon and vegetation, indicated coming conditions of weather.

Although much of the younger generations, less observant than were their forefathers, depend upon the next day's kind of weather by reading or hearing weather forecasts as compiled and disseminated by the U. S. Weather Service, there are still many North Carolina mountain folk who hold fast to the old weather traditions, which have been handed down to them by word of mouth by countless generations.

A new moon on Saturday will bring foul weather.

When swallows fly high, there will be fair weather, but when they fly low, there will be rain.

The dark bands on a wooly bear indicate the severe parts of winter and the light color tells what part of winter will be milder.

When sparrows are noisy after sunrise, fair weather will predominate.

The kingfisher hisses when rain is coming.

Thick husks of corn and hornets' nests built near the ground are omens of a severe winter.

The creaking of chairs and tables indicate rain.

When many cobwebs are seen at morning, the day will be fair.

A rain before seven and an old woman's dance are soon ended.

When crows fly crazily, look for rain.

Unless a storm is already in progress, a rain before seven will cease before eleven.

Sudden rains never last long.

When the robin perches high and sings loudly, the weaher will be fair.

Rain is due when dogs scrape the dirt.

When the sun sets in clear weather and rises the next morning in clear skies, there will be a spell of clear weather.

The number of fogs in August indicate the number of snows during the following winter.

Good crops follow heavy snows during the preceding winter.

It will soon rain when the hills and mountains look higher than usual.

Crickets singing unusually loudly and toads crawling over grass indicate an early rain.

Distant sounds, such as the noise of trains, whistles and bells, heard very plainly, indicate that the weather will be fine.

Ants hustling to their nests are omens of an early rain.

Bats flying in the evening indicate clear, dry weather.

Rain is soon coming when poultry go to roost earlier than usual.

The soot from chimneys and flues fall quickly before an early rain.

As a rule, a halo around the moon indicates rain. A very large halo foretells a storm.

Humid or dry weather during the next twenty-four hours can be foretold by shaking the untanned dry skin of a sheep. If the skin be limp, rain or snow may be expected; if it is crisp, dry weather will follow.

> January snowy,
> February flowy,
> March blowy,
> April showery,
> May flowery,
> June bowery,
> July soppy,
> August croppy,
> September poppy,
> October breezy
> November wheezy,
> December freezy.

When mules kick their stalls or bray more fequently than usual, bad meather is coming; and when bees hurry home and keep close to their hives, flies settle in swarms upon a cow, rheumatic pains hurt worse, and *mare tail* clouds lace the sky, get ready for rain.

Dog Days is the period when Sirus, the Dog Star, rises and sets with the sun.

A month will be wet when there are two full moons in it; a changing moon on Saturday or Sunday will produce changing weather; when there are four phases of the moon in a single calendar month, the weather will be extremely bad; and the month that has no full moon and the month in which the full moon misses Saturday or Sunday only two days will have abnormal weather.

> Red clouds at morning
> Give shepherds warning;
> Red clouds at night
> Bring shepherds delight.

When hogs carry straw or other bedding materials during the day, stormy weather is in the offing.

When a cat washes its paws and feet, there will soon be rain.

A rainbow at morning denotes foul weather, but a rainbow in the evening denotes clearing weather.

When the sun sets behind a bank of clouds on Wednesday, it will rain before Sunday.

Thunder in February indicates that there will be frost on the same date in May.

A full moon at Christmas denotes a poor grain crop the following season.

When a rooster crows unusually early or late, rain will soon come.

A blacksnake in October denotes a mild winter.

Strong winds during cold weather denotes early warming conditions and strong winds during mild weather foretell a fall in the temperature.

When geese pick and wash themselves, rain will soon arrive.

Flocks of crows disappear just before a rain is due.

Mock suns denote windy weather.

When owls hoot in a clear, loud note, fair weather is due.

Ducks quack loudly and appear restless before a storm.

A grumbling sound in the belly of a hound indicates rain.

A Thursday Christmas foretells a windy winter and a dry summer.

When oxen sniff the air or lick their hoofs it will soon rain.

The dark bands on a wooly bear indicate the severe parts of winter, the light bands, the milder parts.

When sparrows are noisy after sunrise, fair weather will predominate.

The kingfisher hisses when rain is coming.

Thick husks on corn and hornets' nests built near the ground indicate a severe winter.

The creaking of chairs and tables foretells rain.

Spiders leave their webs before an approaching storm.

When many cobwebs are seen in the morning the day will be fair.

When smoke settles to the ground, there will be rain soon. When it rises straight up, the day will be fair.

When gnats fly high, the day will be fair.

Rain is coming when chickens go to bed earlier than usual.

When a chicken lies down and stretches itself, there will be thunder soon.

A dove calling indicates that there will be rain within three days. So does the calling of a raincrow.

Thunder before seven, rain before eleven.

The Ruling Days (the first twelve days after Christmas) indicate the general type of weather for each of the twelve months of the year.

When chickens refuse to seek shelter during a shower, the rain will continue at length.

Turtles and terrapins crawling about indicate rain within a very short time.

Kill a snake and hang it upon a limb, stomach upward, and a storm will occur within twenty-four hours.

Night air will cause earache.

Many cobwebs at sunrise indicate that the day will be fair.

Frogs singing in March denote an approaching cold spell. When catbirds arrive, the cold is past and it is favorable weather for planting gardens and corn.

Rain on the first Dog Day is an omen that most of the Dog Days will have rain.

15.
General Superstitions

THE appearance of a comet forebodes a war.
If a live snake be thrown into a fire, its legs will appear.
A whistling girl and a crowing hen always come to some bad end.
It is bad luck to kill a snail or a frog.
A cat kills a baby by sucking its breath.
Tell a dream before breakfast and it will come to pass.
If a crimp comes in the hem of your skirt, you will soon have a new dress.
The white spots on a single person's nails indicate the number of sweethearts the person has.
Lightning never strikes the same spot twice.
A trip or journey should not be begun on Saturday.
Burning a grain of corn will cause the next crop to be a lean one.
Walk a crack in the floor and it will hurt your mother's back. Walk on seven straight and it will heal your mother's back.
If you see a star fall, it indicates that you will soon hear of a death.
For a man to see the wedding dress of the bride-to-be before she dresses for the ceremony brings bad luck and sorrow.
On Old Christmas, the bees turn over in their hives; cattle get on their knees and pray for their owners.
If you are ticklish on your knees, it indicates that you steal biscuits.
Handling warts on someone's hand will cause warts to grow on your hands.
Handling a toad will cause warts to come on one's hands.

Usually, a baby will be born soon before or after the full moon.

A measuring worm on one's clothes is an omen that one will soon receive a new suit or dress.

For a wish to come true, repeat the following verse when seeing the first star at evening:

> Star light, star bright,
> First star I've seen tonight,
> I wish I may, I wish I might
> Have the wish I wish tonight.

For two persons to dry their hands on the same towel at once brings bad luck.

Two persons who wash their hands together will be friends forever.

Drink three cups of water to cure the hiccups.

Swallow a watermelon seed and a plant will grow out of the mouth.

Watching a departing person out of sight brings bad luck to the person watched.

Milk from a woman's breast will cure sore eyes.

The husband should carry his bride over the threshold of their new home in order to guarantee a happy married life for both.

Stepping across a grave will cause the buried person to haunt one.

The child who can kiss its elbow will become a rich adult.

The dream one has in a house first slept in will come true.

An onion planted and named for a baby will prevent the baby's having colic.

16.
Old Superstions Regarding Animals

BITE a mule's ear to tame it.
Handling toads causes warts on hands.
Killing a honey bee brings bad luck.
A blacksnake in October denotes a mild winter ahead.
The cry of a screech owl near one's home denotes the early death of a member of the family.
A cow that gives blood-streaked milk has been bewitched.
A singing cricket in the house denotes good fortune.
A crowing hen, if not killed immediately, denotes dire misfortune.
Carry a rabbit's foot on the person for good luck.
Killing a cat brings the worst of bad luck.
A buzzard's head worn around the neck will cure headaches.
The dragon fly or devil's darning needle sews shut the ears and mouths of naughty children.
More dogs are liable to go mad during Dog Days than at any other period of the year.
When a rooster crows at night misfortune is in the offing.
A cat's breath will kill a young baby.
Houseflies are scavengers of filth.
Rub salt on a cat's head to ward off witches.
When horses kick their stalls at night, thieves are nearby.
A *madstone* from the gall bladder of a deer will cure hydrophobia.
A small flint rock in the firebox of a cookstove will keep chicken hawks from the chickens.

17.

Old Superstitions Once Were Not Superficial

FOR many decades, much of the old superstitions brought into the mountains of Western North Carolina by the early settlers and added to by many of their descendants conditioned the lives of the people. While there were those who scoffed at the old traditions, as there were many in later days, there were large numbers whose lives, surrounded by a maze of superstitions, accepted them as true and allowed the old sayings to profoundly influence their daily activities.

Some of these traditions had originated in England, others had come from Ireland and Scotland, while many of them had been absorbed in New England, Pennsylvania, the Coastal Plain and the Piedmont Region. The Western North Carolinian is of predominately Anglo-Saxon strain and his distant ancestors brought with them much of the folklore of the British Isles, including their home remedies, their stories of ghost-haunted castles and the ghosts that flitted over the countryside.

The Irish remembered their *boogers* and the Scotch had their stock of superstitions.

It is not strange that the North Carolina mountain people had their regional superstitions, for there is regional superstition in all areas of the world. Even the Indian neighbors of the early settlers contributed to them much of their own folklore. Besides, superstition was acquired by the early settlers, no doubt, by *signs* and omens from the loneliness and eerie environment of the rugged topography and the dark shadows which the mountains cast at night. Good luck and bad luck followed *portents* relative to the circumstances and events of their daily life in their strange and lonely environment.

In the early existing environment of almost endless forests, dark coves and valleys, deep shadows on a moonlit night and uncertainty when a pale moon shined, the lone traveler often felt a prickling of the spine whenever an unfamiliar sound occurred or a strange - looking shadow was observed. Anything which was unfamiliar was feared to be a sign, warning, omen or ghost. Only the brave, whose mind was not laden by superstition, experienced no qualm.

The continuing mournful howling of a hound at night was thought to foretell death, and the hound was hastily brought into the house to silence him.

The eerie notes of a screech owl within a hundred feet of a home also was believed to foretell death, and when death happened coincidentally or soon afterward, the woman of the house sang,

"When you hear the scrooch owl hollerin',
Somebody's dyin', Honey,
Somebody's dyin'."

It was thought by some persons that the bird could be driven away by a member of the family removing his shoes.

Transplanting a pine tree was considered an ill omen. It was believed that when the tree became sufficiently large "to shade a grave," death of a member of the family would come to fill it.

Catching the first sight of a new moon through the branches of an oak tree or over one's left shoulder foretold dire misfortune, unless one turned, saw it over the right shoulder and made a wish.

It was thought that a child's turning a chair on one leg in the house would cause his or her ears to fall to the floor.

It was believed to be bad luck to bring a hoe into the house.

A covey of quail thundering out of the brush as one is on the way to make a trade signifies a loss will result in the deal.

To prevent toothache, the toenails and finger nails should be cut only on Friday.

In building a fire, name it for a sweetheart. If the fire burns readily from the use of a single match, the sweetheart is true.

Place a poker or flatiron in the fireplace to stop an owl from hooting.

Friday falling on the Thirteenth of a month is a very unlucky day.

Bad luck will come to the three persons who light their cigarettes or pipes from the same match.

One should leave a house by the same door entered to avoid bad luck.

To prevent hawks bothering chickens, put a pebble from the spring in the ashes of the fireplace.

Seeing a white horse is an omen of good fortune or unexpected happiness.

Finding and wearing a four-leaf clover brings good luck.

Tieing a knot in the fragile yellow vine proves that a girl's lover is true.

An unmarried man or woman can prove whether a sweetheart is true by being able to hold a burning match until it is completely consumed. One may grasp the burned end with the fingers, without breaking the ash, while the first end burns.

After eating a teaspoonful of salt without drinking liquid immediately before going to bed, a girl will dream of her intended husband.

A girl can see her future husband by staring several minutes through a tumbler filled with water at a mirror on the opposite side.

It was believed that a baby's teething might be hastened by rubbing its gums with a minnow very recently hooked from a nearby river or creek.

A small bag containing onion skins, when worn around the neck, was thought to ward off croup and several other diseases.

To cure chickenpox, the patient was made to lie upon

his face while a flock of chickens were chased over him. The greater number of fowls running over him, the quicker would be the recovery.

A flannel string worn around one's waist under the other clothing was thought to make one immune to pneumonia.

One *cure* for warts was to steal and bury a dishcloth Another was to make a notch in a buckeye stick, bury the stick, and when it decays, the warts will vanish. Still another was to bury beans under the eaves of the house so deeply that they would never sprout.

To cure the croup, the patient was made to drink a cupful of pork grease.

The old superstitions and traditions began dying long before the paved highways and the secondary roads made easy and quick transportation possible and removed most of the isolation from the beautiful North Carolina highlands, which once were hostile and almost inaccessible to all but the hardiest and most courageous people. Good schools and the media of communication have enabled the people to reach the glorified heights which, by dint of bravery, determination and planning, they have won for themselves.

Walking with one shoe off and one shoe on was believed to foretell a day of ill luck for each step the unshod foot touches the floor or ground.

For the wife to spill salt while working in the kitchen denoted that she and her husband would soon quarrel.

Friday was believed to be the fairest or foulest day of the week.

Any scratch or other body wound during Dog Days was thought to be more liable to develop blood poisoning than at any other time of the year and it was believed that August 27th was the *most poison* day of all.

For a man calling on his sweetheart to place his hat upon a bed in her home was considered a sure omen that they would never be married.

In some communities it was considered bad luck to sing at the table. Children who did so before seven

The hag prepares a brew.

would cry before eleven.

Some families never burned discarded shoes or clothing, because this was believed to result in a burn on the body of the owner.

Good luck in raising baby chicks was thought to be obtained by tossing the hatched eggshells over an outbuilding.

It was believed an omen that a guest or guests were coming when a housewife accidentally dropped her dishcloth upon the floor.

A black rooster crowing before an open door, unless the door was slammed shut immediately, foretold the death of a member of the family.

Despite the number of self-styled *doctors*, there were many home remedies that were practiced.

18.
Magic Formulas

HOW TO BLOW FIRE FROM A BURN OR SCALD

A CONJURER who had learned the secret from a non-relative was thought to be able to blow fire from a burn or scald, if not too severe, by blowing repeatedly for several minutes upon the burned spot, while mentally repeating the following verse:

> Two little angels from the West,
> One named Fire and one named Frost,
> Go away Fire!
> Come, Frost!

FORMULA FOR STOPPING BLOOD

The *blood doctor*, usually a woman who had *sufficient* faith in the formula, stood before the patient and recited several times, if the usual three did not stop the bleeding, in a loud, clear voice Eziekel 16:6:

"And when I passed by thee, and saw thee polluted in thine own blood, I said unto thee when thou wast in thy blood, Live."

FORMULA FOR REMOVING WARTS

The wart conjurer gently rubbed each wart, sometimes using spittle, while repeating in an inaudible whisper:

> This old wart ain't come to stay;
> It'll start leaving on this day.
> It must leave, so I say
> "I'll just throw this wart away."

FORMULA FOR BECOMING A WITCH

The candidate for becoming a witch carried a black cat and a loaded rifle to a large iron pot already placed at the fork of a small stream flowing toward the east, killed and boiled the cat until the flesh dropped from the skeleton, then she threw the bones into the stream. One bone floated upstream and the devil got it. She then climbed to the top of the nearest high mountain, waited until sunrise and yelled loudly: "Devil, devil, my soul is yours! Place your mark upon my body and make me a witch!" Then she shot the sun with her rifle.

HOW TO PREVENT BEING BEWITCHED

Before a witch could bewitch a person, members of his family or his stock, she had to borrow something from the family. To prevent witchery, nothing must be loaned to the witch.

A WITCH DOCTOR'S FORMULA

To overcome witchery and punish the guilty witch, the witch doctor must draw a picture of the suspected witch with a charcoal upon a large chip of wood, place it in the fork of a small white oak tree and shoot it with a silver bullet.

HOW TO UNBEWITCH MILK

Put a quantity of the bewitched bloody or ropey milk in a shallow vessel and whip with a bundle of small switches until all the milk is emptied from the vessel. This not only unbewitches the milk, but causes blue stripes to appear on the witch's back and thighs.

FORMULA FOR MAKING A GHOST SPEAK OR DISAPPEAR

The persons seeing or hearing a ghost woud say three times: "In the name of the Almighty, what do you want? Either speak or go away."

(Usually it was the frightened person, not the ghost, who rapidly disappeared from the scene.)

FORMULA FOR RIDDING A SLEEP-WALKER OF A WITCH

It was once thought that sonambulists were being ridden by witches and the formula for ridding the sleepwalker of the witch was to shake him roughly while repeating this formula:

> Witch, witch, go away I say;
> You won't ride this one today.
> With sorrow and care and a sigh,
> Ay, unsaddle this person and fly!

WITCHES' FORMULAS FOR CHANGING THEIR FORMS

Note—It was thought that all witches had what they called *familiars*. When they found it convenient to change their physical forms, they recited secret formulas. Some of the *familiars* were cats, rabbits, blackbirds or other forms or animals or birds.

For changing herself into a cat, she would say:

> I shall go into a cat,
> With sorrow and sigh and a black shot;
> And I shall go in the devil's name
> Ay, while I go home again.

When ready to change herself into her human form, she repeated this formula:

> Cat, cat, the devil send you care;
> I am in a cat's likeness just now,
> But I would be in a woman's likeness
> Even now.

FORMULA FOR PREVENTING A NIGHTMARE

> Matthew, Mark, Luke and John,
> The bed be blessed that I lie on.

A Wagon Threads the Mountains, 1775

FORMULA FOR DISPOSING OF A SMALL EGG

(Sometimes a hen laid a very dimunitive egg which was thought to be an omen of impending bad luck and to circumvent the threatened misfortune, the egg was held in the right hand, the person turned his back to the wall of the dwelling house and threw the egg over his left shoulder and the roof, after repeating this rhyme:)

>Bad luck egg, bad luck egg,
>I throw you over my shoulder
>To prevent all the bad luck
>You might have brought.

FORMULA FOR INDICATING ONE IS A WITCH

If a woman, when leaving another's home, recited this verse, it was thought she was a witch:

Matthew, Mark, Luke and John,
Saddle the cat and I'll be gone.

FORMULA FOR MAKING A TABLE TALK

The table should be small, light-weight, preferably unvarnished and a size that will seat four persons. Four persons seat themselves, with the palms cupped downward, the fingers touching one another and remain silent for several minutes or until the palms feel moist. The hands lie lightly on the table and no one uses hands or legs to encourage the table's rising on two legs.

The leader begins by commanding, "Rise, Table, rise and talk," and continues the command until the two legs begin rising. As the table rises, the pressure on the table should be decreased, then questions and commands may be given by any person at the table. Although a limitless variety of questions may be propounded, they may include such as "Table, strike once for the number of years I have lived;" "Strike the date of the month;" "How many times will I marry?" "How many children will I have?" "What will be my age when I die?" etc.

Don't attempt to cause the table to rise or strike by pushing on it and do not be discouraged if the first experiment fails.

Sometimes, after long experiments, the table will rise at almost the first command and, with all hands held several inches above it, the table will continue rising until it must be pressed upon to prevent its capsizing.

19.
Children's Rhymes

RHYMES AND JINGLES RECITED TO SLEEPY CHILDREN

Eeny, meeny, miney, moe!
I caught a lizard by the toe;
If he holler, let him go;
Eeny, meany, miney, moe.

As I went down the new-cut road,
I met Mr. Possum and I met Miss Toad.
Every time Miss Toad would jump,
Mr. Possum would hide behind a stump.

Trot, trot, trot!
I spilt my buttermilk every drop.
A ribbon of red, a ribbon of black;
I tied them so tight they'll never come slack.

Baby Bunting up in the tree top,
When the air moves the cradle will rock;
When the wind blows the cradle will fall;
Down will come cradle, baby and all.

Big Tom Daly, Little Tom Daly,
Two pretty wives and three little babies.
One got drunk and one got drownd-ed;
One ran away and they never found him.

One and two and three and four,
Feed the cat and close the door;
Four and five and six and seven,
All good children go to heaven.

When the wind begins to roar
Like a lion at your door;
When the door begins to crack
Like a hickory on your back;
When your back begins to smart
Like a penknife at your heart;
When your heart begins to fail
Like a ship on sail;
When the ship begins to sink
Like a bottle full of ink;
When the ink begins to spill,
Then the sow will go to mill.

Bye, bye, Baby Bunting,
Your daddy's gone a-hunting
To get a rabbit skin
To wrap my baby in.

The Queen was in the cupboard
Eating bread and honey,
The King was in the closet
Counting out his money,
The maid was outdoors
Hanging out the clothes,
Along came a blackbird
And nipped off her nose.
    (Nips the child's nose.)

(Touching each toe with finger, patting little toe)
This little pig says, "I'll steal wheat."
This little pig says, "I'll go, too."
This little pig says, "Where?"
This little pig says, "I'll go tell."
This little pigs says, "Wee, wee, wee. I'm so
   little I can't get over Granpap's door sill."

(Tapping each toe with fingertip, patting little toe)
Shoe the old horse, shoe the old mare;
Drive a nail here, drive a nail there,
But let the frisky little colt go bare.

CHILDREN'S LOVE VERSES PASSED IN SCHOOL

Roses are red, violets are blue,
Lilies won't tell that I love you.

The sea is wide and I can't step it,
I love you and you can't help it.

As sure as the grass grows round the stump,
You are my sugar lump.

Love me, Babe, love me true,
Love me, Babe, as I love you.

Crosses are for kisses,
As you know, my dear;
If you long for kisses,
You will find them here.

As sure as the stars shine up above,
It's only you I'm bound to love.

Don't tell another girl of this,
Because it's you I wish to kiss.

Violets are blue, roses are red,
And I'll love you until I'm dead.

Apples are good, peaches are better;
If you love me, you'll answer this letter.

If you love me as I love you,
No knife can cut our love in two.

When Grandpa (Grandma) was younger than you,
He (She) loved a girl (boy) not as sweet as you.

Roses are red, violets are blue;
If you'll love me, I'll love you.

As sure as the squirrel has a bushy tail,
My love for you will never fail.

On the road to Asheville, 1880.

ROPE-SKIPPING RHYMES

Jimmy gives me candy
Almost every week,
Jimmy followed me to school
And kissed me on the cheek.
   (Repeated until there was a miss.)

Papa loves Mama,
Mama loves me,
If I had a sweetheart
Happy would I be.
   (Repeated until there was a miss.)

PREPARATION TO KISSING A SWEETHEART

Over latch, under latch,
It takes good kisses to make a match.

20.
Misquotations From the Scriptures

MANY quotations from Scripture and those not in Scripture have, for generations, become folklore, as the following will show:

"That he who runs may read." "That he may run who readeth." —Hab. 2:2.

"God tempers the wind to the shorn lamb." See Isaiah 28:8.

"Owe no man anything but love." "Owe no man anything, but to love one another." —Romans 13:8.

"Exalted to heaven in point or privilege." Not in the Bible.

"In the last days, summer cannot be distinguished from winter." —Not in the Bible.

"In the midst of life we are in death." —From a hymn of Luther.

"It is always the innocent who suffer." —Not in the Bible.

"Bread and wine which the Lord hath commanded to be received." —From the English Catechism.

"Men shall become weaker and wiser." —Not in the Bible.

"A nation shall be born in a day." Isaiah 71:8 reads, "Shall a nation be born at once?"

"Not to be wise above what is written." —Not in the Bible.

"The merciful man is merciful to his beast." "A righteous man regardeth the life of his beast." Proverbs 12:10.

"As iron sharpeneth iron, so does a man the countenance of his friend." "Iron sharpeneth iron; so a man sharpeneth the countenance of his friend." —Proverbs 27:17.

"Prone to sin as the sparks fly upward." "Born into trouble, as the sparks fly upward. Job 5:7.

Second Samuel 18:9 makes it plain that Absalom's head, not his long hair, was caught in the boughs of the tree and Genesis 2:18 says that Eve was Adam's help meet, not his *helpmate*.

21.
The Early Vernacular of the North Carolina Mountains

NOT all the old-time speech of the early people of North Carolina mountains and their descendants for many decades consisted of held-overs from Chaucer's and Shakespeare's days, but much of it did. Some of it was due to mispronunciation, a syntax of non-English origin and a deliberate diction which was meant to fit the culture and environment of the strong and daring people in their splendid isolation. Much of it, however, was the colorful and spicy speech of the Elizabethan era.

The earliest settlers were either people from the English Isles and other Northern European countries or their descendants who had been born in America. Besides the English, there came the Scotch-Irish, the Germans, Dutch, with some Welsh, with those of almost pure Anglo-Saxon blood having predominance in number. They intermarried, lived for generations almost without the printed page, flavored their language with the idiom of Chaucer and clung tenaciously to the picturesque language of the days of Good Queen Bess.

It should not be forgotten that the English language itself is an idiom of West German.

As time passed and contact with the outside world was lost, the metamorphis of language gradually continued, as has always been the case when mountain ranges, bodies of water and other natural barriers isolate groups originally speaking a common language. It is a historic fact that the Latinic Languages of Southern Europe derived their strength from the Latin of the old Roman Empire after Rome collapsed and lost contact with its former far-flung provinces, hidden beyond mountain range and river. Doubtless, had progress moved less rapidly, the mountaineers of the Appalachians and Blue Ridge eventually would have had a language not understood by the English-speaking *out-landers*, but two centuries was too short a period for the completion of the metaphoric process.

Just as Gullah, a dialect along the shore and on the islands off the coast of South Carolina, has lasted more that 250 years, but will soon be a dead language, so is the picturesque speech of the North Carolina mountains rapidly giving way to language uniformity imposed by many factors, including good schools and colleges, an abundance of printed matter, the radio and television and contact with the outside world.

The phraseology and syntax of the early people of North Carolina mountains was doomed around the turn of the century, when the State's Literary Fund and the treasuries of the mountain counties made a longer school term possible, but for a decade or two the language of the most isolated rural regions was little affected. The slow process of eradication continued with marked success as the years passed and newspapers, magazines and books became more plentiful and high schools were established. Colleges began to dot the area. Those who observed closely knew that the purists of our language and the traits of mankind to conform were winning.

Today one has to travel farther and search more diligently than formerly to hear the old 'dialect spoken, but a part of it still exists, more or less, in many secluded neighborhoods, remindful of Chaucer's and Shakespeare's language.

Any area has its localisms and colloqualisms, as well as mispronunciations of many words, but nowhere else in all the world—not even in England—were they blended and mixed so colorfully for so long a time with the spicy diction of the Elizabethans as they were on the tongues and lips of the stalwart men and women of the North Carolina mountains.

Perhaps the many factors, including the work of the purists of our English language, have accomplished less than many persons think.

Following is a partial glossary of early mountain vernacular:

a-childing — gestating; pregnant.
aingern—onion.
ain't losin' any sleep over hit—not worrying about it.
a chunk of a gal—a medium-size girl.
a give-out—an announcement.
air—are.
appearant—apparent.
a preach—a sermon.
arm baby—child small enough to be carried in the arms.
auger-eyed—sharp eyed.
atter—after.
at the getting place—where usch things are obtained.
a whoop and a holler—a considerable distance.
ain't had much schoolhousing—hasn't had much formal education.
as all get-out—very much so.
ast, ax—ask.
a wheel—a silver dollar.
awnt—want.
bad off—very ill.
bad mouthed—using obscene or profane talk.
bald faced whiskey—whiskey fresh from the still.
bait—a good meal.
benasty—degrade.

beyant—beyond.
biddy-peck—to nag mildy.
bigging and bigging it—exaggerating.
biggety—self-esteemed; too haughty.
big room—family room.
big sight—much or many.
birthed—gave birth to.
blamyfied—to eternally blame without reason.
blockader—a distiller of illicit whiskey.
breaking—failing by age.
bodiaciously ruint—seriously injured.
broke in—trained for definite acts or works.
biscuit bread—biscuit; wheat or rye bread.
bug days—days which should be avoided when planting potatoes to prevent bugs from destroying the green leaves.
budget—package.
butter-mouthed—speak flattery.
buttock down—sit down.
calm of day—early broad daylight.
can't confidence—can't trust or believe.
carry—escort.
carry on—to act foolishly or immorally.
catawampus—crosswise; big. and fine.
cat heads—biscuits.
chunk-washer—a heavy rain.
clim, cloom, clome—climbed.
confisticate—confiscate.
coon's age—a long time.
coon-a-long—walk on all fours.
cooter around—to walk aimlessly or idly.
corn-fed—husky; strong.
cowcumber—cucumber.
crack of day—break of day.
critter—a riding mare; a wild or vicious animal.
danced in the pig trough—remained single after an older brother or sister had married.
day down—late afternoon.

doctor-medicine—prescribed by a doctor; not a home or herb remedy.
doctor-woman—a midwife or female herb doctor.
do-me-sol-ray—fitting or suitable.
don't dig up old dead cats—don't recall disagreeable subjects; don't bring to mind old dislikes or hatreds.
done nothing out of the way—did no wrong or immoral.
doney-girl—a female sweetheart.
don't set well—doesn't please; make angry.
drave—drove.
drink some water and suck our thumbs—eat a scant meal.
drooped up—disappointed in love; ill or indisposed.
druther—prefer.
druthers—preferences.
edzact—to reason out.
et—ate.
every bit and grain—all, entire.
everyday gal—steady sweetheart;. jusem sweet.
exclamations for expressing diverse surprises—For goodness' sake! For heaven's sake! For the land's sake! Good gracious alive! Go on! Did you ever! Did you ever hear the like! Great day in the morning! I'll swan! I'll be John Browned!. Mercy me! Not since Heck was a pup! My goodness! My stars! Sakes alive! Shut your mouth! You're kidding! Great snakes! Great guns! I wish that I might die! What do you know! I wish I might drop dead! Holy Moses! Holy smoke!
feather-legged—cowardly.
feet sot to run—ready to hurry away.
ferment—opposite.
fireboard—the mantel.
fish or cut bait—trade or drop the subject; put up or shut up.
do your work or quit your job—fight or stop quarreling.
fit, fout—fought.

flat and cold—unconcious; entirely; without any more to say.
fleshen up—to put on weight.
fram—beat.
fotch—brought.
fotch on—opposite to store-bought; homemade; delirious.
frayed—fretted and cried, as a baby; was restless.
frazzled—very tired.
friz—froze.
funeralize—preach a funeral sermon.
fur—far.
fur piece—quite a distance.
fur side—farther side.
furder—farther; further.
furdermost—farthest; furthermost.
gap—a mountain pass.
garden sass—vegetables.
gayly—well; recovering from illness.
giving tongue—barking or baying loudly.
gommed—messed; disarranged; ruined.
got his (her) hips up—became offended.
got a mash on—in love with.
go-poke—a traveling bag.
gormed, gaumed—messed up.
got the big head—very highly self-esteemed.
granny woman—a midwife.
graveyard cough—a tubercular cough.
greasy doors—doors of a family who have recently slaughtered hogs.
gritted bread—grated green corn meal.
gumption—judgment; good sense.
half-cocked—very impulsive; capped and ready to shoot.
ham-meat—pork ham.
handful of days—very few days.
handful of minutes—very few minutes.
has other fish to fry—has other work or activities.
hant—a ghost that haunts a definite place.

happyfing—happening.
heisted—lifted or raised.
hell a-hooting—trouble starting; feuds; serious quarrels or fights in progress.
hoofing—walking.
hog-killing time—rowdyism; festivities; gayety; quarreling or fighting.
hollow, holler—cove between ridges.
holp, holped—helped (old English form).
home-boys—boys and men of the same neighborhood.
hopping mad—very angry.
house plunder—furniture for the home.
how the land lays—how the situation, condition, etc. appears.
goozle—to speak hoarsely; to swallow rapidly.
goozler—a boy whose voice is changing.
handy—quick; nearby.
hot shots—first whiskey that comes from the worm of a still.
huh?—what?
humdinger—very fine; something well done.
I can't come it—I can't eat more.
I'm a knowing—I know.
not sure for certain—not certain or sure.
infare—wedding feast given in the groom's home.
ill—of explosive temper.
It don't please me none—it gives no pleasure.
heard the wind blow before—heard boasting before; don't believe it.
jair—a jar, to jar.
jairy—nervous.
Jim-swinger—a frock or long-tailed coat.
jubus, juberous—dubious; frightened.
jularker—a male sweetheart.
kicked the bucket—died.
kiver—cover.
knee child—a child small enough to hold on the knee
laid by—had intended; cultivated for the last time.
lap child—a child that could be held in the lap.

laying off—intending.
let's play like—let's pretend.
lick-splitting—walking rapidly.
light and hitch—come in and visit.
light in the breech—frail.
lit a rag—left hurriedly.
littlest-un—the least child in the family.
made a preach—preached a sermon.
make the fur fly—fight another fiercely.
make the chips fly—work hard; be industrious.
mealy-mouthed—too timid to speak frankly.
meeting-house—church.
middling peart—fair in health.
might-nigh—almost.
mincy—finicky.
misdoubt—doubt.
mizzle—to rain lightly in small drops.
mommick—mess, impair or disarrange.
mulligrubs—to be upset.
nairy—none.
narr—narrow.
neighbor-people—neighbors.
nothing doesting—laziest; idlest.
notorious republican—notary public.
not worth a hill of beans—worthless.
not worth talking about—of no value.
on the down-go—declining in age or health or economic status.
ouches—aches; pains.
out of the head—delirious; crazy.
outen—extinguish; put out.
old-timey—old-fashioned.
painter—panther.
pap—father.
peart—lively; in good health.
perzactly—exactly.
picking down—becoming worse.
picking up—improving.
pile up with trash—live with the low class or immoral.

pimeblank—exactly.
pinked in—late afternoon came.
pitch a fit—to fuss or rave in anger.
play-purty—a toy.
pooch out—to extend.
preacher-man—preacher.
pump knot—knot on the head from a blow.
pure forgot—entirely forgot.
purely don't pleasure me none—doesn't please or satisfy.
purely likes to eat—really likes to eat.
purely lay the hickory on—whip soundly with a switch.
put up or shut up—trade or drop the subject; fight or stop threatening.
quod—quoted.
riding critter—a horse for riding; not a draft horse.
right smart—a good deal.
rifle-gun—rifle.
rimtion—a great deal.
rip and tear—to raise cain.
riz—arose.
risin—a boil, carbuncle or stone bruise.
rooster a gun—to cock a gun.
rosm—resin or rosin.
runction—a quarrel or fight.
ruinate—ruin; degrade.
ruther, druther—wish; desire.
saprising time—youth.
satisfactionate—satisfy; satisfactory.
sapsuck—sapsucker; a half-wit.
sassafrac—sassafras.
scrooch up—slump the shoulders; take less room.
setting rounders—ones sitting near; idlers.
setting chair—chair.
shagnasty—a low bred person.
shut-in—gorge.
since Heck was a pup—a long while ago.
shammuck—to walk.
short talk—quarrelsome talk.

skun—skinned.
slaunchways—slanting.
slicks, hells—heath balds or tangled rhododendron thickets.
smidgen—a very little.
smooch—to kiss.
slow-poke—one who walks or works slowly.
sow-belly—side meat or bacon.
smart and sassy—in high spirits.
smackdab—exactly.
snuck—sneaked.
snurl—to curl the lips.
spraddle—straddle.
spang—exactly.
sparking—courting; wooing.
spindlingest—slenderest.
store-boughten—store-bought.
sull-up—pout.
swag—a sag or depression.
sweethearting—dating or courting a sweetheart.
tater riffle—light bread.
techious—easily riled.
the slows—the habit of moving very slowly.
to contrary—to vex or anger.
chance on—happen on.
tooth-dentist—dentist.
toting papers—a criminal warrant.
trade—shop or buy.
traipse—walk aimlessly or needlessly.
trees air springing green—trees are leafing.
turn right-handed—turn right.
turn left-handed—turn left.
turkey tails out—spreads out.
turned the stomach—nauseated.
'twant nothing—amounted to nothing.
twistificated—twisted; danced.
twistification—a dance.
two curves and a cuss fight—the distance beyond two curves of the road and to the next house.

A Cascade Near Warm Springs, 1875

using around—dating or courting a sweetheart.
varmint—any creature, especially a wild animal.
weepy-eyed—tearful.
what will you take for it and not back out? what is your exact price?
whitleather—cured but untanned hide.
whitleather stage—at the age of an old maid.
whole lot—a great amount.
whup—a whip; to whip.
woodscolt—a child born out of wedlock.
yan—yonder.
yan side—the farthest side.
yearth—earth.

22.

An Old-Timey Sparkin'

(Written in old Mountain Folk Speech)

JAKE. Here I am, Nancy, atter a-licksplittin' hit from beyant the Bushy Mountain, through a chunkwashin' and ' gully-makin' rain, to larn that you have another jularker, when all the time I had sez to myself, sez I, "Effen a feller ever had a jusem sweet that he could confidence hit war you!" I didn't awnt any ever-day gal but you,, an' now I feel I don't have a chanct.

Nancy. Shet up, Jake He ain't confiscated me yit, an' that by a big sight.

Jake. Hearn that spraddle-legged new jularker of yourn fotch you a nickel's wuth of stick candy an' youns set on the front porch an' et hit atwixt times he war a-smoochin' you. I wish I might drap dead if I can stand sich goin-ons. I war a-feelin' gayly until I larned you had gommed up our sparkin' matters, not a-knowin' what war a-happyfyin' right under m' nose — might nigh smackdab an' pimeblank under my nose! I'm hoppin' mad, Nancy!

Nancy. Huh?

Jake. I said I'm hoppin' mad, an' I'm not sure fer certain that ye'll lay yer eyes on me agin fer a coon's age. Hit don't pleasure me none to git in sich a jam— an' don't ye misdoubt that.

Nancy. Who glabbed to you 'bout my doins?

Jake. The preacher-man war fust, then the neighbor-people let the cat outen the poke. I purely liked you, Nancy; thought I war rootin' whar the acorns war in a-tryin' to find myself a home-wife. I'm right smart disappinted that ye went back on yer promises in a middlin' peart way. I'd bet a pewter button that yer new jularker is not wuth talkin' about, much less wuth a hill of beans.

Nancy. Yer outen your head, Jake.

Jake. Ye've ruinated our sparkin', an' hit is jist the sap risin' part of our lives. I didn't awnt nary other jularker a-usin' round you. I don't awnt any other jularker sweetheartin' you. I thought the bug war a-hoppin' high atwixt us, but apperantly hit warn't, Nancy. I wonder me why ye been a-steppin' out on me. I didn't awnt ye to do that.

Nancy. I ain't a-losin' no sleep about yer awnts, Jake. Yer a-takin' hit hard, ain't ye? Yer all scrooched up like yer bad-off.

Jake. Yeahr, I'm all drooped up, Nancy. I feel like I drave my ducks to a bad market. I've shore run into lots of trouble this mornin'. I'd nearly druther die than go through with this agin, but I'll soon hoof hit back home.

Nancy. Ye already got yer feet sot to run, Jake?

Jake. Effen I had my druthers, I wush I'd never met a ficety gal like you. Ma allers has said I don't have no gumption.

Nancy. Ye got yer hips up bad, ain't ye, Jake. I'm a-knowin' ye feel jist tol-able. Le's play like we're still good friends.

Jake. I want t' ax ye one thing, Nancy.

Nancy. Ax hit.

Jake. Hit's a likely question. Do you love me a smidgen yit?

Nancy. I ain't a-faultin' ye, Jake, for axin' that question. Times I recall ye axed me that lots. Ye've helped me to be happy, Jularker Jake. O' course, I love ye a smidgen. I love ye a rimption.

Jake. I've heard the wind blow before.

Nancy. Nary a time, Jake, since I wuz a knee child, have I been guilty of biggin' an' biggin' hit. That feller I traipsed with to the meetin'-house yistiddy to hear the preacher-man funeralize the corpse war my cousin from Tennessy who war a-footin' hit to his uncle's home be-

•99•

yant the county line. Kaze he war a furriner, neighbor-people thought he war my new jularker; meetin'-house goers 'magined hit; all the settin-rounders in the meetin'-house thought so, too. Everybody might nigh drave me out of my head a-starring at we-uns. Mebbe that war why I thought the preacher-man made a bad preach. I'm a-feelin' smart an' sassy today, ye war jealous, an' I awnted ye to sull up more. I jist awnted to contrary ye a smidgen, fer I got a mash on ye, Jake, an' I thought ye had a mash on me. Don't dig up no more old dead cats, fer hit don't set well with me. Hope I may die effen I didn't jist awnt to see how the land lays atwixt us. I'm glad ye ain't mealy-mouthed when ye think I'm done ye wrong. I got my enjoys by a-seein' ye pitch a fit. I guess ye wort t' a hit me smackdab in the face fer calf-ropin' ye along, but ye did look weepy-eyed. Air ye still jumpin' mad?

Jake. I 'pologize; 'twant nothin'.

Nancy. Yer appearantly peartenin' up, ain't ye, Jake?

Jake. Yeah, I'm a-straitenin' up as all git-out, but I come might nigh a-bein' bad-mouthed. Les play like we've never had a sparkin' fuss nur fout 'bout nothin'. I - I'm in good speerits now. I 'low yer the sweetest cake of maple sugar in the woods. Times I recall, when ye warz jist a chunk of a gal, I longen to smooch ye then. Scrouge up, Jusem Sweet an' let me buttock down beside ye an' buss ye forty times. Hit's come on that I'm a-lovin' ye s'much that I don't intend ye to go unhitched till ye reach the whitleather stage and be on the cull list. While my love fer you is a-pickin' up, I don't awnt yours to be a-pickin' down.

Nancy. Don't ever say farewell to me, Jake.

Jake. I'll never say farwell to you, Jusem Sweet, if I can holp it.

23.
Proverbs and Expressions

Pay fifty cents for what he thinks he is worth and lose money.
 He is eating high on the hog.
—He would climb a tree to tell a lie rather than stand on the ground and tell the truth.
 He and the devil drink through the same straw.
• Life is short and full of blisters.
 As poor as Job's turkey.
• He can stay longer in one hour than any person I know.
 He would rather tell a lie on a credit than tell the truth for cash.
 He didn't walk in his father's footsteps because he couldn't spraddle far enough.
 Close the door. Are you from North Carolina?
 He will marry when the wrong girl comes along.
• Get while the getting is good.
 Handle women and glass with care.
 Why try to keep up with the Joneses, when they're trying to keep up with themselves?
 Don't take a mouthful too big to swallow.
 He crawfished out of it.
• His mouth is no prayer book.
 He needs it as much as a hog needs saddlepockets.
 As uncomfortable as the seven-year itch or cracker crumbs in the bed.
 Would skin a flea for its hide and tallow.
 So lazy he wouldn't work at a pie counter.
 Grinned like a possum.
 Before they married, he acted as though he could eat her, but now he acts as though he wished he had eaten her.

Every rooster scratches toward himself.
They can't afford to butter both sides of their bread.
Squeeze the dollar 'till the eagle squalls.
When you can't afford it, dont butter both sides of your bread.
He smelled a mouse.
As little sense as a goose.
Small potatoes and few in a hill.
Can't see an inch from the end of his nose.
A spoonful of sense.
Her tongue is loose at both ends and has a roller in the middle.
Not as much chance as a one-legged man in a relay race.
If you like music, get married and play second fiddle.
As slick as greased lightning.
As scarce as hen's teeth.

24.

Early School Rules

UNTIL late into the first decade of the present century when the school system was operated by the individual counties, most rural schools were taught in small one-teacher schoolhouses or neighborhood churches, and pupils from the ages of six years to twenty-one years were legally allowed to enroll. The average cost of a schoolhouse in North Carolina in 1900 was only $153.00 and the average salary of white teachers, which exceeded that of black teachers, was $24.79 monthly for four months of the year.

The schools were ill-equipped. Long benches, many of them without backs, instead of desks, were used. The blackboards were crudely fashioned of planed boards, mounted on two legs nailed to the back and painted black. Pieces of sheepskin were used as erasers. Nearly all pupils used slates in lieu of paper.

At best, most of the teachers could boast of only the equivalent of a fair seventh grade education. Only a few had attended one of the academies scattered throughout the mountains and fewer still were college-trained. Between school terms, they were employed in other work activities; such as farming and saw-milling. A small minority taught two-week writing or singing schools or served as pastors of scattered churches.

The schools were ungraded and the pupils were classified as primary, intermediate and advanced. There were no report cards, no system of grading achievement and pupils promoted or retained themselves.

A store in each rural school district was designated as a school book depository, where books might be purchased by parents or pupils. Many older pupils bought only a small number of books, usually those which they preferred to study, for they were allowed to study as few or as many as they wished. There were those who equipped themselves with only one or two books, studying, say, arithmetic one term, then another subject the following term. Many older pupils were eager to learn, while others attended school only to enjoy the social and recreational features available. There were those who enrolled in order to be with their sweethearts or to escape work on the farms.

In many instances, the difference in age groups constituted problems. Teachers were on the alert that love affairs between the sexes of the older pupils were held to a minimum. The older pupils, if they wished, might spend only a part of each school day in the classroom; the young men were allowed to visit stores and the post office in the afternoon or visit a swimming hole in a nearby river or creek, being required only to answer roll call as the last feature of the day.

The male pupils occupied benches on one side of the aisle, while the female pupils sat on the opposite side. The school body was seated according to size, beginning with the smaller pupils on the front seats.

Because of a dearth of writing books, teachers set copies for most pupils at intervals during the day.

Every school had a few troublesome pupils, most of them being the larger boys, and because of this, it was necessary for the teachers to maintain strict rules. Whipping was usually the form of punishment and many teachers began the term by having a supply of switches, varying in size from small to those almost as large as fishing poles, stacked in a corner of the schoolroom. The teacher seldom smiled during the school day and punishment for infraction of the rules was certain. Sometimes he chased a large boy almost a quarter mile down a road before being able to administer the switching. Often the boy outran him.

On the first day of school, after Scripture was read and the Lord's Prayer recited, the rules were given, sometimes orally, at other times requiring them to be written by the older pupils. While not all teachers had the same set of rules, the following are examples of common ones:

Don't do any sparking or writing love letters in school.

You shall not hug or kiss or play kissing games on the school grounds, in the schoolhouse or when walking to and from school.

You shall not play *Whip* or *Winding the Ball of Yarn* when both boys and girls are in the game.

Go no more than a quarter of a mile from the schoolhouse when playing *Fox and Dog*. Boys and girls cannot play the game together. When the game is played by the girls, the boys will engage in *town ball or double bats* in the front yard or a nearby field.

Neither boys nor girls must wink at one another.

Boys shall not carry any girls in their arms or on their backs, unless heavy rains or mush ice have made the creeks and branches impossible to cross because of flooded footlogs; and then, only boys who are barefoot or wearing boots may do so. No hugging, squeezing or kissing shall take place while the girl is being transported across the water.

No chestnuts, haws or apples will be eaten in time of books.

Don't pretend to see ghosts or hants in an effort to frighten the younger pupils.

Don't whisper across benches during school hours. If you must speak to someone, snap your fingers for permission.

Hold up your hand when you wish to go outdoors, but don't forget to take advantage of the recess periods.

You shall not throw snakes, frogs or worms or any other live creature upon another boy or girl, and don't frighten anyone by pretending to do so.

You shall not fuss or fight. Remember that I am the only person in this school who is paid to fuss and fight and this is costing the county twenty-five dollars per month.

You shall not go in swimming in a naked state within 200 yards of the schoolhouse, the wagon road or a dwelling house.

Do not curse or swear.

Do not attend the school when you have the itch, but remain at home and diligently apply to your body a mixture of lard and sulphur or bathe yourself in poke root ooze. Even at home, you must not swear when the poke root ooze burns your hide.

Chew yellow root when you have sore mouth.

You shall not bring to school any hawk's claw for use in pinching the ears and noses of others; neither shall you stick others with pins or chestnut burrs. Don't attempt getting by by sticking pins in the toes of your shoes and hurting others, then show your empty hands in order to prove yourself innocent.

You must not put grains of corn, isinglass, asbestos or other objects down the collars of others to cause their backs to itch or squirm.

Do not put any dead pigs, polecats or other dead animals in the schoolhouse loft to create a stink.

You shall not argue hotly as to whether the earth is round or flat.

25.

Old Popular Songs and Ballads

Mountain people have always liked to sing, whether sole or in groups or the accompaniment of banjos, fiddles and their musical instruments. String bands, especially at dances, musical festivals and the old time fiddlers' convention have been among their greatest enjoyments. Before the advent of the phonograph, radio and television, it was customary for the family to gather around the hearthside or meet in a neighbor's home at night and sing old English ballads and other ballads, religious songs, hymns, even love songs. For decades, the old Christian Harmony Songbook was a favorite in home, church and at singing conventions. Love songs and ballads expressing sadness, tragedy or triumph were preferred and at dances when string band and vocal music were in order, the dancers seemed to step more lightly. Girls and women sang as they donned their clothes at morning, prepared the day's meals and did their daily chores; men often sang as they plied their axes.

Many of the old songs and ballads are with us today, and many of those which originated in the mountains continue to gain more popularity.

PUT MY LITTLE SHOES AWAY

Mother dear, come, bathe my forehead, for I'm growing very weak;
Mother let one drop of water fall upon my burning cheek;
Tell my loving little schoolmates that I never more shall play;
Give them all my toys, but, Mother, put my little shoes away.

Chrous:
I'm going to leave you, Mother, so remember what
  I say;
Oh, do it, won't you? Mother, put my little shoes
  away.
Santa Claus he gave them to me, with a lot of other
  things,
And I think he brought an angel with a pair of gold-
  en wings.
Mother, I will be an angel by, perhaps, another day;
So, I'm asking, dearest Mother, put my little shoes
  away.

Soon the baby will be larger, then they'll fit his little
  feet;
Oh, he'll look so nice and cunning when he walks
  along the street.
Now I'm getting tired, Mother; soon I'll say to all,
  good-day;
Please remember what I tell you—put my little
  shoes away.

THE OLD ARM CHAIR

My grandmother she, at the age of eighty-three,
One day in May was taken ill and died,
And after she was dead, the will, of course, was read
By a lawyer, as we all stood by his side.
To my brother it was found she had left a hundred
  pounds,
The same to my sister, I declare,
But when it came to me, the lawyer said, "You see
She has left to you her old arm chair."

Chrous:
How they tittered, how they chaffed,
How my brother and my sister laughed
When they heard the lawyer declare
Granny had only left to me her old arm chair.

I thought it hardly fair, still I said I did not care,
And in the evening took the chair away:
The neighbors they me chaffed, my brother at me laughed,
And said, "It will be useful, John, some day,
When you settle down in life, find some girl to be your wife,
You'll find it very handy, I declare.
On a cold and frosty night, when the fire is burning bright,
You can sit in your old arm chair."

One night the chair fell down; when I picked it up, I found
The seat had fallen out upon the floor,
And there, to my surprise, I saw before my eyes
A lot of notes, two thousand pounds or more!
When my brother heard of this, the fellow, I confess,
Went nearly mad with rage and tore his hair,
But I only laughed at him and slyly whispered, "Jim,
Don't you wish you had the old arm chair?"

SWEET CIDER TIME WHEN YOU WERE MINE

When it's harvest time, my sweet Angeline,
We will wander through the golden grain,
Like a meadow lark, just before the dark,
We will harmonize our love refrain.

We shall harvest all our dreams together,
And we'll reap a heap of happiness divine.
Just a step from town, we shall settle down,
When it's harvest time, Sweet Angeline.

Chorus:
Same old quail a-whistling, whistling in the lane,
Same old fragrance from the new-mwn hay.
Like the oak tree yonder, our love will remain.
Angeline, I love you more each day.

Twilight shadows falling, all the chores are done,
Ma and Pa a-rocking to and fro;
Two gray heads together, two heart beats as one;
He sang to her this song so soft and low.

THE ORPHAN GIRL

"No home, no home!" cried an orphan girl
At the door of a rich man's hall,
As she trembling stood on the polished stone
And leaned on the marble wall.

Her dress was thin and her feet were bare
And the snow had covered her head.
"O, give me a home," she feebly cried,
"A home and a piece of bread.

"My father, alas, I never knew;"
Tears dimmed her eyes so bright;
"My mother sleeps in a new-made grave,
'Tis an orphan that begs tonight."

The night was cold and the snow still fell,
As the rich man closed his door,
And his proud lips curled with scorn and said,
"No bread, no room for the poor."

The rich man lay on his velvet couch
And dreamed of his silver and gold,
While the orphan girl in her bed of snow
Was murmuring, "So cold, so cold!"

The morning came, and the orphan girl
Still lay at the rich man's door,
But her soul had fled to the home above,
Where there's bread and room for the poor.

TOM DULA

Hang down your head, Tom Dula,
Hang down your head and cry;
You killed poor Laura Foster
And now you're bound to die.

You met her on the hilltop,
And God Almighty knows,
You met her on a hilltop
And there you hid her clothes.

You met her on the hilltop,
You said she'd be your wife:
You met her on the hilltop
And there you took her life.

Chorus

Hang down your head, Tom Dula,
Hang down your head and cry;
You killed foor Laura Foster
And now you're bound to die.

OLD DAN TUCKER

Old Dan Tucker was a fine old man,
He washed his face in a frying pan.
On Christmas morning he got drunk,
Fell in the fire and kicked up a chunk
    Get out of the way, Old Dan Tucker,
    You come too late to get your supper.

Old Dan Tucker ate raw meal
And combed his hair with a wagon wheel;
He gave his neighbors the squarest deal
And died with toothache in his heel.
    Get out of the way, Old Dan Tucker,
    You come too late to get your supper.

BALLAD OF FRANKIE SILVERS

(Frankie Silvers, the first woman to be hanged by North Carolina, was executed in Morganton on July 12, 1833, for the murder of her husband.)

This dreadful, dark and dismal day
Has swept my glories all away;
My sun goes down, my days are past,
And I must leave this world at last.

Oh, Lord: What will become of me?
I am condemned you all now see.
To heaven or hell my soul must fly
All in a moment when I die.

Judge Daniel has my sentence pass'd,
These prison walls I'll leave at last,
Nothing to cheer my drooping head,
Until I'm numbered with the dead.

But oh! that dreadful Judge I fear;
Shall I that awful sentence hear,
"Depart thou cursed down to hell
And forever there to dwell?"

Farewell, good people, you all see
What my bad conduct brought on me—
To die of shame and disgrace
Before this world of human race.

My mind on solemn subjects roll;
My littlee child, God bless his soul!
All you that are of Adam's race,
Let not my faults this child disgrace.

KIDDER COLE

(Superior Court Judge Felix E. Alley, who died in the '50's, lived in Cashiers Valley, Jackson County, and until he began studying law, was a good banjo musician. He also loved to dance. When he was sixteen years old, he began writing the banjo ballad, Kidder Cole, at a dance one night in Cashiers Valley, adding to it as the months passed. The star of the ballad was a mountain beauty of his neighborhood with whom he was in love. At an all-night dance, young Alley was late in arriving and found that his cousin, Charley Wright, a larger boy than he, was already dancing with his sweetheart and, as his heart burned with jealousy, began writing the first stanzas of the ballad. Over the months, he added to the original, playing them on his banjo.

Kidder Cole did not become the wife of either Alley or Wright, but the ballad has gained in popularity over the decades, spreading from Grimshaw in Cashiers Valley over the entire mountain area.)

My name is Felix Eugene Alley;
My best girl lives in Cashiers Valley;
She's the joy of my soul
And her name is Kidder Cole.

I don't know—it must have been by chance—
'Way last fall when I went to dance,
I was to dance with Kidder the livelong night,
But got my time beat by Charley Wright.

So, if ever I have to fight,
I hope it will be with Charley Wright,
For he was the ruin of my soul
When he beat my time with Kidder Cole.

When the dance was over, I went away
To bide my time 'till another day,
When I could cause trouble and pain and blight
To sadden the soul of Charley Wright.

I thought my race was almost run
When Kidder went off to Anderson,
Where she had gone to school,
Leaving me at home to act the fool,

But she came back the following spring
And, oh, how I made my banjo ring.
It helped me to get my spirits right
To beat the time of Charley Wright.

Kidder came home the first of June,
And I sang my song and played a tune.
I commenced with all my might
To put one over on Charley Wright.

I did not feel the least bit shy
On the Fourth of the next July
At the head of a big delegation,
I went to attend the Fourth celebration.

When the speaking was over, we had a dance,
And then and there I found my chance
To make my peace with Kidder Cole
And beat Charley Wright, confound his soul!

Charley came in for an hour or so,
But seeing me with Kidder, he turned to go
Back to his home with a saddened soul,
For I had beat his time with Kidder Cole.

Oh, my little sweet Kidder girl,
You make my head to spin and whirl;
I am yours and you are mine
As long as the sun and stars shall shine.

Oh, yes, my Kidder Cole is sweet,
And it won't be long until we meet
At her home in Cashiers Valley,
Where she'll change her name to Alley.

I like her family as a whole,
And I'm especially fond of George M. Cole.
I believe I shall like to call him *Pa*,
When I get to be his son-in-law.

Some of her folks I don't like so well,
But I may sometime, for who can tell?
And, after all, between me and you,
I'm not marrying the whole derned crew.

The French Broad Below Asheville, 1875

26.
Yates Radford, Typical Mountaineer

THE color and fabric of rural life in the Carolina Mountains, as the first decade of the Twentieth Century marked its halfway point, were known by those who knew Yates Radford, his home and his interests. It is true that life differed in detail as the colors, size and shape of the scraps of a patchwork quilt differ in the composite whole, but the pattern was almost the same. The isolation for decades had caused the social and economic life, the folkways and the folk speech, even the architecture and furnishings of the homes of most of the people to run to a pattern. Yates Radford had been born in the mountains, had spent his years in the rugged region, and he was typical of the mountaineers of his day.

Although there was a slightly perceptible blend of Scotch-Irish and German, his heritage was predominately English. In his veins ran purer Anglo-Saxon blood than could have been found in most places of the British Isles. His speech was partly that of the days of Shakespeare and Chaucer, but it was colored by a strange and racy dialect which had originated in the mountains. His vocabulary and phrases were as strong and expressive and as rugged as the spirit of the people of the mountains about him. He had descended mainly from the yeoman class in England and in the Western North Carolina Mountains, like his ancestors, he tilled only a small acreage, but the bread that the sweat of his brow brought him and the freedom and hope that were his had elevated him to the gentry of the mountain breed about him.

He was sturdy, self-reliant and courageous, as were most mountaineers of the isolated area. In pitting his strength and imagination against the forces of nature, his instinct, almost as strong as that of the fowl whose wings beat a pathway through the air to a nesting place halfway around the world, told him what the laws of survival demanded. Instead of wealth, he dreamed of the necessities and comforts of life for himself and his family; a plenteous supply of food in variety; clothing suitable for all the seasons; shelter from the rains that swept forest and field, the howling winds and snows of winter; home-furnishings that answered his family's needs; and love and happiness and contentment with his lot when the long day's work was done.

"What more than these should a man want?" he sometimes asked himself.

There were many other things than these that a man would need and want, but they had not come to the mountains or into Yates Radford's dreams.

He was deeply religious, attended to his own affairs and was not aggressviely belligerent, as a rule, but once he had *settled the hash* of a lowlander dude who had laughed at his syntax and dialect. He could neither read writing nor write reading, except his scribbled signature, but had learned to read print haltingly by skipping the hard words he ran into. At that, he read in an amusing manner, as did most adults of that day. As he read his Bible and almanacs, he ran a finger under each word and pronounced it in a barely audible monotone in order that his lips and ears might vouch for what his eyes thought they saw.

He was very superstitious, mistaking folklore for scientific knowledge. The superstitious beliefs by which he had conditioned his life during the part of the Nineteenth Century would cling to him through his fractional part of the Twentieth Century.

He planted his crops, butchered his hogs and nailed the shingles on the rafters of his buildings according to the phases of the moon and the signs of the zodiac.

Often the phase of the moon did not coincide with the sign of the zodiac on the dates that he thought his crops should be planted, then he studied his almanac and calculated the nearest date between the days. Although he respected the signs of the zodiac, he believed that the phases of the moon were more important for planting most of his seeds and roots. His general rule was to plant the crops that bore their fruit above the ground on the light of the moon; that is, when the moon was increasing from new to full; and the crops that bore their fruit below the ground were to be planted on the dark of the moon; that is, when the moon was decreasing. When potatoes were planted on a favorable phase of the moon and the sign of the zodiac concurred, the vines, he said, would be low and the potatoes large and plentiful; but planting them on the light of the moon would produce tall vines and small potatoes. Corn planted on the dark of the moon, he argued with the few persons who disagreed, produced tall stalks and very slender ears that stood erect, while corn planted on the light of the moon produced a heavy crop of large, drooping ears.

His life was conditioned by numerous good luck and bad luck signs, by the dreams that he dreamed and by the weather omens which he read in the sun, moon, stars and clouds. The twinkling of the stars denoted early changes of weather conditions; a sun-dog indicated radical changes of atmospheric conditions; and the cusps of the moon told whether to expect dry or wet weather.

"It will be a wet month," he said, "when there are two full moons in it. Look out for crazy weather when the moon changes on a Saturday or Sunday and when a calendar month has four phases of the moon. When a month has no full moon or when the full moon misses Saturday or Sunday only two days, the weather will be foul. It will be the same when the new moon comes on a Saturday."

He, like most mountaineers, felt that the mountains were part and parcel of his being; that God seemed nearer on a montain top than He did in a valley or in the lowlands. That was why he had built his home on a mountainside; why, when the opportunity presented itself, that he climbed a high peak to view the splendor of a sunrise or sunset; to view the winter stars or contemplate the panorama of tangled ridges and towering peaks about him.

As a Confederate soldier, he had known much of the lowland country, but he had never revisited it afterward. He wished to experience the exciting beauty of the highlands and the things which they possessed. He thrilled when the scent of springtime, curiously fresh and sweet, filled his nostrils and when the fogs of summer dampened his face. His heart was light, however hard his duties, when October painted the foilage of the forests in magic colors of scarlet, yellow and gold; and when the dry leaves of mid-autumn crackled and snapped under the soles of his boots, he thought it excitingly joyful. He got his enjoys by tramping a *fur* piece with his dogs beside him, through the bare forests denuded by the winds of early November or when winter snow had changed the leafless twigs and branches of shrub and tree into what seemed to be a veritable fairyland. On winter nights, as he heard the winds roar through the mountains and down the ridges, he closed his eyes in peace and comfort, making believe the winds were packs of roaring, hungry lions, hard put to find their quarry.

As he toiled, he thought and dreamed and planned. He had seen the mountain area increase in population, the economic and social conditions markedly improve; the culture, which had peculiarly fitted the mountain people, was changing slowly. He realized that it was not enough that his people had established an almost self-sufficient economy and yet lacked so much which the outside world possesed. Although the few roads which led from one community to another and the fewer that led to the outside world were being improved, they were still narrow, crooked and steep dirt roads which were impassable during heavy rains and snows or when the rivers and creeks they crossed were clogged with ice. He realized that the isolation would have to be overcome in order that transportation facilities would be available for carrying their products of farm and forest to distant markets. Local consumption assimilated only a small fractional part of the real potential of the farmland and the greater part of their natural resources could not be profitably exploited. Schools, at least, equal to many he had seen outside the mountains, should be established. He dreamed of the many who would eventually come into the area to enjoy the scenery of the land, when traveling was more convenient and comfortable. As he toiled, he dreamed, and he knew that the dream books which he consulted had no interpretations for the dreams that came to him in his wakeful hours. He was aware of the fact that many mountaineers were dreaming dreams of the same warp and woof as his, but he realized that they were long, long dreams. From men who had traveled extensively throughout the area and from first hand knowledge, he knew that most of the mountain people were ambitious and industrious, strong of effort in assaulting the rugged land, and carrying within their hearts dreams which they dared not reveal in full. He knew that the mountaineers belonged to a breed of hardy, self-reliant and stalwart people whose greatest enemy to be fought was the isolation in which they had been pocketed for generations. Had he known that many persons outside the mountains were accusing most mountaineers of being apathetic and lazy, he would have resented it fiercely.

Hospitality and neighborliness characterized Yates Radford, as they did all mountain families. A traveler of another community, caught in a storm or finding darkness approaching, was given meals and a bed for the night. No stranger seeking lodging and food for the night was denied the comfort that he sought.

It was a social custom, especially during winter months, for families to make unannounced and uninvited visits in the homes of their neighbors to while lonely evenings away, and this was no exception in the home of Yates Radford. Conversation, the telling of ghost stories and witch tales, games by the younger folk and bits of gossip were always in order. Apples and nuts, sweetbread and apple cider, called snacks, instead of refreshments, were available in plentiful supply.

Except for size, Yates Radford's home, which had four rooms, was typical of most homes in the mountainous country. It was constructed of well-hewn logs, the cracks between them being daubed with red clay, and a huge chimney made of selected field rocks stood at either end. The inside walls and joists were ceiled with planed puncheons and the floors and partitions which separated the rooms were made of the same kind of handwrought materials. Although the architecture was of the pioneer type and the exterior and interior had the appearance of good workmanship, it had been built for utility and comfort more than for beauty. The thick walls made for warmth in winter and for coolness during hot weather.

While the whipsaw was common and a few sawmills were beginnnig to dot the region, making lumber available to those who could afford to build framed houses or to cover the outside walls of log houses to make them to resemble weatherboarded framed buildings, Yates Radford preferred the appearance and strength and stability which the log house possessed. Too, he thought the log house was a symbol of the strength and stability of the mountains, his own spirit and that of the pioneers and their descendants.

The heavy doors were hung on wooden hinges and had latches of wood, instead of doorknobs. From the latches, through a small hole in the doors strong cords or leather strips, called latchstrings, hung outside. No visitor knocked on the door for admittance, for everyone in the mountains was familiar with the old rule that said, "Just pull the latchstring that hangs outside the door."

Yates Radford utilized every square foot of space in his home. He had no closets, but the family had made out pretty well without them. In the walls of his home he had bored auger holes and inserted pegs of seasoned locust on which hung a great variety of items. In the family room, which served as kitchen-dining room-living room, hung strings of beans dried in the hull, ears of seed corn, red peppers, fly-specked dried apples, bridles, hanks of yarn, gourds, bags of seeds for the next season's planting, ropes, rawhide boot and shoe strings, bunches of medicinal herbs for treating minor ills, the fly-brush, fly taps and fly traps, dried pelts of small furbearing animals, bags of copras and dye materials, almanacs and dream books, two rifles, the shot pouch, a powder horn and a comb case. The comb case contained a single large horn comb, which all the family and guests used.

On the walls of the three bedrooms hung bags of feathers for replinishing pillows and featherbeds, the family's apparel which was not presently in use, chains and unused towels. In one end of a small bedroom sat Aunt Millie's loom and on the walls about it hung other hanks of yarn and tow.

The loft, which was reached by a ladder from the family room, held boxes of onions, threshed beans, shelled corn, tanned hides, small tools, shoemending materials, wooden shoe lasts, clothing and footwear to be repaired, discarded clothing to be used for patching and dish cloths, and other items.

In the walls of the long porch were other pegs for holding barrel hoops, horseshoes, plowshares, traps, bunches of homegrown tobacco, a bag of Indian relics, and pelts stretched upon boards for drying. The joists of the porch, bare of ceiling, contained hoes, quilting frames, axe handles, bed slats, the apple stirrer, rakes and fishing poles.

The house stood on a site which had been only partially graded, which provided plenty of space beneath half the floor. The stone wall foundation and a pole partition made two large low rooms, one of which was a kind of catch-all. In it were plows, ox yokes, scythes, knot mauls, a spinning wheel, a grindstone, some ladders, drawing knives, a bench on which shingles were shaved, a broadaxe or two, an old bear trap, a large barrel used for scalding butchered hogs, a froe, calf muzzles, gimlets, augers, some sheep shears, a discarded trundle bed, and a few empty bee hives. The other compartment was reserved for hens' nests and the picking of ducks and geese. Sometimes a sow and her pigs were temporarily penned there.

Yates Radford's household furniture was strongly built. The bedsteads were built of four-inch oak; the rails were about twenty-four inches from the floor and had large auger holes spaced at intervals for containing the cords upon which were placed a straw or shuck mattress, a feather bed, blankets and quilts and a decorative coverlet. The chairs and rocker were sturdily built of hickory and had seats of woven hickory splints. The bureau resembled a modern dresser, had greater dimensions, but no mirror. Made of oak and varnished well, it was a beautiful piece of furniture. The wooden cupboard was made to fit the corner in which it sat; the dining table was much wider than those of today and contained a large drawer for storing dishes of food which had been left from a previous meal. A bench, instead of chairs, was used between the table and the wall. A partitoned chest for holding meal and flour had a bushel or more capacity. A small hand mill, held between the knees, was used to grind the coffee after the green beans had first been parched in an iron skillet. A gourd dipper in the wooden water pail was utilized by the family and its guests as a common drinking cup.

His old wooden-wheeled clock, an heirloom which had come into the mountains with his first ancestor who had chosen the Carolina Mountains as a home, had not run for years, but that fact made little difference in his day's schedule. So regular were his habits and so keen his observation that he could tell the time within a quarter hour by sun or moon or stars, when the sky was clear. The dusk and the dawn, the crowing roosters and his own body were his timekeepers.

The people who knew Yates Radford knew the color and fabric of general rural life of the Carolina Mountains when the Twentieth Century was young.

27.
The Tuckahoes

TUCKAHOE was the name given by the American Indian to an edible tuberous vegetable or underground fungus that grows in Eastern North Carolina and is small, knotty and inferior to other potatoes. In the Carolina Mountains the appelation was given to a person who was lazy, shiftless and lacking sufficient ambition to improve his economic condition to the point of raising his standard of living.

Zeke Tillet, by all the standards of mountain society and its definition of the word, justly merited the epithet of Tuckahoe; albeit the appelation of the name for a person followed the pattern of mankind's trait of laying on ugly descriptive expressions when conformation to the ideals of established society is ignored or violated. By Zeke's day, the epithet had become smooth and ready on the tongues of those who felt themselves as engaging more courageously and strenuously in the fierce struggle against the then hostile environment of the isolated highland region.

Although there were other mountaineers who sometimes squirmed under the same brand, whether Zeke cared at all, one way or another, there was none who ever knew. Neither he nor his neighbors had heard or read Emerson's words, "In some way, every man on earth is my superior." Therefore, this philosophy entered into the thinking of none of them.

In passing judgment upon Zeke, his neighbors had taken into consideration the fact that he had done little or nothing to improve the large acreage of rich bottomland, black-soiled coves or surrounding ridges or mountainsides which was his by inheritance. Another score against him was due to his having taken no wife, although there were many good and beautiful young women in the countryside just spoiling to be married.

There had been large fields, which his father and grandfather had cleared and cultivated, but the forests had reclaimed most of them. One small patch of land seemed sufficient to grow all the vegetables and roasting ears which he needed. His corn meal and flour were obtained from the neighborhood's miller in exchange for dried ginseng or pelts of wild animals which he trapped and hunted. He bartered the same items of exchange to the merchants and the ginseng buyer for groceries and other staple necessities.

"I don't intend to dig myself half to death, when man's needcessities are so few," he once told a neighbor. "Along with wild meat, honey, ramps and branch lettuce, it requires only a little garden sass and store-boughten food to satisfy nourishment for the body. Without planting a seed or a root, a man could live well in these mountains, if he would only take each season by the horns.

"My eyes get hungrier for beauty than my stomach does for food. That is why I plant many kinds of flowers around the house and my doorway. After the cold and snow are gone, there's nothing that satisfies my spirits so much as seeing the first wild flowers in bloom. The fresh sweet woodsy smell of spring in my nostrils excites my soul. I purely like to follow the scent of bursting bud and young green leaves, as I search for the earliest violets, lambtongue and puccoon flowers on the sunniest side of the ridges and in the deep coves.

"Spring is like a teasing, fussy woman, at first. I guess it's because spring don't come to the mountains according to the almanac. It sometimes mixes sunshine and snow flurries, rain and clear skies, cold and warm weather, violets and frosts, as though uncertain whether to remain or go away again; maybe it's just teasing. When winds howl and late snow flurries come, while the sun hides its face behind a cloud for an instant, then smiles again, spring reminds me of a fussy woman. But when the poplars are springing green, I know that spring is really here. Sap-rising time is a time to rejoice."

Zeke lived alone in the three-room log house in which he and his parents lived before their death. He prepared his meals, kept house, laundered and patched his clothes, repaired his furniture as needed, whistled as he went about his chores. He made his sweeping brooms from the broom-corn which was grown in his garden, and he scoured his bare floors with a scrub broom which he had made from a section of a hickory sapling by using his knife and fingers in turning one end of it into a brush of thin splits, as did most rural mountain families of the then and there.

He spent many hours fishing the small river which ran through his land and the many creeks and branches. On many days at the right season of the year, he chased the wild bee to its nest in a hollow tree upon the mountainside. It was fun to drop a sticky bit of cotton upon the bee, then let his keen eyes follow it toward its hive.

Every year he went to the swamp in the small hollow which was watered by a buried spring branch, where he knew that the early warmth and the moisture of the swamp first set the grassblades growing; and there he sat on a small boulder, shoes and socks off, and let the airblown grass spears tickle his bare feet, while he joyed in the swelling buds of shrub and sapling.

When the hot days of summer came, he often visited a deep area of water, where the river curved around the end of a jutting ridge, divested himself of all his clothing, then swam and dived until he was refreshed and his skin tingled. For hours sometimes, he sat on a rock at the river's edge and dangled his feet in the rippling water, as he watched the dragonfly dart past and birds and squirrels drink from the crystal water.

He hunted birds' nests, sometimes stooped to kiss the flowers which he passed and played with the cunning blacksnakes.

He knew that a surprised blacksnake would glide away for a little distance and then, because he is a curious creature, would stealthily crawl back to watch the one who had surprised him. As he spied the blacksnake's return, he would exclaim: "Oh, there you are, old fellow! I knowed that you would be back."

Next to exploring his wide acres in a seemingly aimless fashion, he liked best to tramp over the land in autumn, when the crisp leaves crackled under his feet and the ripe nuts scattered the ground. He delighted in watching the gray squirrels and chipmunks carrying chestnuts and walnuts to their winter storehouses.

When Indian summer permeated the mountains and the harvest moon flooded the evenings in brilliant beauty, he sat on a rail fence, graying with age, that wormed its way across a ridge and through what was once a well-kept apple orcharrd. Occasionally, woodchucks stole through the dusk: to nibble on the few knotty apples upon the ground and to these Zeke sometimes called: "You lucky fellows! Instead of storing your winter food in holes and hollow trees, as do the squirrels and mice, you store your food under your skins."

Zeke was very superstitious, as were many persons of that day. One belief in particular, that the weird cry of a screech owl near a home indicated that a member of the family would soon die, clung to his mind tenaciously. It was a part of the folklore of much of the mountain region that, on the night Frankie Silvers had murdered her husband and burned his body in the fireplace, a flock of screech owls sat in the trees surrounding the cabin and sang their shivering songs all the night through.

Once a man of another neighborhood asked to buy a good-sized tract of land on the southern end of Zeke's estate, but was refused the offer.

"I don't need the money," Zeke told him. "Anyway, I've riz at calm of the day too many times over the years just to watch the sunshine play with the fog in them woods to consider selling a foot of that land."

Knowing Zeke's pet superstition, the man said in a final effort to clinch the trade: "The woods down there are filled with screech owls."

"Scrooch owls or no scrooch owls," Zeke replied, "I ain't selling that land. I've already insured myself against scrooch owls by cutting down every bush and tree within two hundred feet of my house."

The hot days of mid-August had reddened the berries of the ginseng plant until it was possible for a man with keen eyes to walk a mountainside slowly and discover the herb that grew within a distance of thirty feet on either side of him. And Zeke, wise in the lore of the woodlands, armed himself with his narrow ginseng hoe and a bag and began his annual assault on the treasure of the forests.

It was the second day of his gathering ginseng that started a chain of events of tremendous importance to Zeke and temporarily knocked a part of his philosophy, as many mountaineers expressed it, "onto the main line."

He was prying loose a ginseng root from a crevice in a rock formation when his eyes caught sight of some shiny particles dislodged by his hoe.

"Mica!" he exclaimed, as he examined the material. "The real ruby kind."

He had seen mica that had been dug from two of the largest producing mines in the county, had heard of its processing for sale, but had only a vague idea of its value. He also knew that a mica buyer of Ohio, who was a former resident of the mountains, had been in the area a week in the business of purchasing a shipment for his company there.

With his hoe, Zeke feverishly dug and pried for more than an hour, then he gathered the few sizeable blocks removed from the feldspar vein and hurried home. He sat on the porch, trimming and splitting the blocks into thin sheets, until the setting sun touched only the tops of the highest mountains, then he carefully placed them in an empty flour bag and carried them inside.

Next day, with pick, crowbar and a sledgehammer, he trudged back to his find on the mountainside and resumed his prospecting until he was satisfied that the deposit was very promising. As he trudged back to his cabin, for once the birds and wild flowers were forgotten in the excitement of his discovery.

Early the next morning, he crammed his pockets with dried ginseng for the merchant and placed a few pounds of his best mica in a bag for showing to Buchanan, the Ohio buyer. Barefoot and with his frayed trousers rolled to the knees, because of the heavy dew upon the weeds beside the pathway, he walked with light heart and light footsteps. Sometimes he whistled an imitation of the catbird's call; sometimes he hummed the plaintiff words of a ballad.

In the store yard, the mica buyer was talking with two or three men. Dressed in his city clothes, with carefully polished shoes, and smoking a cheroot, he looked as sharp as the pin that glittered in his tie. Zeke might have described him as looking like a fashion plate, only he had never heard the term. He had meant to say howdy to the men, but none seemed to have seen him, as he passed into the store.

"Sure, my company pays me five dollars a day and expenses while I'm here transacting business for it," Zeke heard the mica buyer say. "I would receive a big bonus, if I could lease or buy a good mica mine in this area."

"So that's how prosperous the man who years ago had operated a small grist mill has become," he told himself. "I guess it's a fact that money can really do big things for a fellow."

The merchant gathered and placed on the scales the ginseng roots as Zeke emptied his pockets.

"What you got in that poke, more sang??" he asked.

'Nope," said Zeke.

"Then, what is it?"

"Mica, I guess."

"Mica?" The storekeeper pulled two or three sheets from the bag and examined it. "Where did you get this?"

Zeke stood silent and cracked his knuckle joints, as

was the custom of many mountain men when they were pondering what to say.

"Where?" repeated the excited merchant.

"On one of my mountainsides."

The merchant, holding several sheets in his hand, dashed to the door. "Look-a-here! Mica! Ruby-colored mica!" he yelled. "And Zeke has lots more of it in a poke."

The group of men hurriedly entered the store, and the buyer held several sheets between his eyes and the door.

"Ruby mica," he said; "and no specks, no flaws. As fine as I've ever seen."

He examined the contents of the bag before speaking again.

"I'd buy a ton of this right now," he said. "Fact is, I'd buy the entire mine where this was dug."

"There ain't no mine there," Zeke explained. "Just a hole, where I've been sprospecting a little lately, but I'm sure they's lots and lots more there."

"If you will allow me to take a few men there and prospect for a week or two, I'll pay you for the mica dug, then lease or buy the mine, if the vein is promising."

"I don't like the idea of gomming up my land with diggings," replied Zeke, "but I recon we might reach an agreement."

"No false promises, but that mine could easily bring you thousands of dollars."

A metamorphis began in Zeke's philosophy. The lust of the flesh and the pride of the eye took hold of him, as the false god of riches and avarice waved a golden scepter before his eyes and quickened his imagination. He forgot the birdsong and beauty of spring, the woodland where the sunshine and fog played among the trees at early morning, the old rail fence upon which he sat when the harvest moon swung in the Indian summer evenings and chided the woodchuck for eating his decaying apples, the wealth of exciting contentment as he watched the migrating geese, and the peace of heart that came when the soft snow clung to and turned into a fairyland the spruce hemlock. But he remembered that, with the riches which came from the mica, he would still have his land. And, besides, he could have as flashy clothes as the buyer wore; he could build a home as large, perhaps, as the courthouse; and enjoyment would come in just counting the money that would be his. During the week that the buyer's hired men brought block after block of mica from the yawning hole, Zeke's daydreams grew to higher piles than that of the mineral. So busily did he watch the laborers work and so steadily were his visionary notions woven that he ignored the wonders of nature about him; he was unaware that autumn was sending its first notes in the form of falling buckeye leaves, that its arrival was near or that the golden rod and blue asters, summer's last love letters, had already been posted.

At noon on Saturday, the buyer was satisfied.

"We shall ride over to the county seat on Monday in the Groverton livery stable's hack," he told Zeke, "and have the legal papers made. Ten thousand dollars on the barrel head, and my company owns the mine."

The ride to the county seat was the most enjoyable that Zeke had experienced. A wagon was the only vehicle ridden before. The spirited horses and hack seemed to glide over the dusty, rock-strewn road. The buyer might have hired a buggy, instead of the large vehicle, for his company was paying the bill, but his eagerness to create an impression of importance and opulence upon others had dictated the manner of his travel. Frequent stops were made along the way. Wherever men loitered at a country store, the travelers halted and the buyer purchased cheroots and other small items. People stared at the buyer and Zeke and attempted to take their measure. The buyer, dressed in his best, and Zeke in his patched clothing, created curiosity wherever they stopped.

Once, when the horses were allowed to rest in the shade of an overhanging tree, Zeke announced that he intended to take a dip in the nearby river.

"I'll go along and watch you swim," the buyer said. After divesting himself completely of his clothes, Zeke climbed upon a ledge of rock and dived into the deep water.

"As graceful as a bullfrog!" exclaimed his companion. Zeke appeared to be in his natural element, as he swam with masterful strokes the length and breadth of the deep water. When his swim ended, he observed that the buyer had removed his footgear and was dangling his feet in the water.

"I did this very often and swam, too, when I lived in these mountains," the man explained. "Not for many years have my feet been in water deeper than my bath. I think, when I left this region, I got away from the best things of life. For a long while after I began living in the city in the lowlands, I felt that something had died inside me. I longed for the mountains, the high cliffs which the clouds sometime touch in passing, the old swimming holes—everything, including the friendly people.

"I longed for the shaded coves where, in the springtime, I would sit and listen to the chorus of birdsongs; the foxes that barked on the ridges haunted me; and the call of the crow near a cornfield sounded in my memory. I would lie awake at night and dream of the rain splashing on the fields of corn, the rasping song of the katydids, the owls hooting from trees in the darkness, and the bees gathering honey where the wild roses bloomed. Even the wooly bear caterpillars, by which I once predicted the coming of winter's weather, often entered my thoughts. I craved to be once again where I could wander idly where the ferns and the lichens grew and the wind rustled peacefully among the corn blades. But I had to work. I became obsessed with my position with the mica company and in providing the good things for my wife. She is gone now. Slowly I climbed to the responsible position I now occupy, but the old things and the old life that I once knew in the mountains have been almost irresistible."

They entered the hack and the driver jerked the reins of the horses. Suddenly the driver turned to Zeke and in nostalgic tones asked: "Did you ever call doodlebugs from their dens in the dust under sloping rocks?"

"Many are the times that I've done that, especially when a boy," Zeke replied, with a surprising laugh.

"Have you teased the catbirds and the bluejays?"

Zeke replied in the affirmative, without changing the wording of his answer.

The man beside him was silent, seemingly lost in revery, for several minutes.

At the county seat, a lawyer soon had the legal papers ready and the buyer handed Zeke the check.

"Ten thousand dollars is a lot of money," the lawyer said, scanning Zeke's unshaven face and shabby clothing. "Better go to the bank and deposit most of it."

"I'll deposit most of it," Zeke replied; "but I'll buy myself some flashy clothes and a pair of shiny shoes and—and—some cheroots. I'll take a thousand dollars with me. I want to feel it, run it through my fingers, count it and try to realize how much ten thousand dollars is."

The buyer accompanied him to the bank and explained to the cashier Zeke's wishes.

"As you say, Mr. Tillet," said the cashier. "What denomination bills do you wish?"

Zeke looked puzzled.

"One's, two's, five's, tens—"

"Dollar bills," said Zeke. "I want to know what a thousand dollars looks like."

The cashier went to the vault and returned with an armful of currency.

"Gosh-a-mighty!" Zeke exclaimed. "How will I ever tote this much? It's enough for every man in the neighborhood."

The cashier laughed heartily.

At that moment, a catbird in a bush outside began trilling its varied notes, as though the happiness of the world was in his heart.

"Let the money lay there a minute," Zeke said. "I want to hear that catbird sing."

"Me, too," said the buyer.

Both men rushed to the door and stood entranced until the bird finished its silvery notes and moved on.

Zeke returned to the cashier's window and, with his hands outstretched in a pushing movement, as though warding off a sinful thing, spoke bluntly and impassionately.

"Put this money back with the rest of it, until I call for it."

Outside the bank, Zeke muttered, "Maybe, I'm crazy."

"And maybe, you're not," his companion said sympathetically.

Zeke had seated himself in the hack when the buyer thought of something.

"Wait here," he said, "until I go across the street and send a wire to my company, informing it of the lease."

He soon returned and seated himself beside Zeke, directly behind the driver.

"Do the fern fairy rings still grow in the grass on Bald Knob?" the erstwhile buyer asked.

"Yep,' Zeke replied.

"And does the lightning still strike its summit and plough furrows in the ground during summer storms?"

"Never misses during July and August. It's worth climbing the mountain to see the ploughing that the lightning has done. People still say, 'Let's climb old Bald Knob to see where God A'Mighty has done His ploughing.' "

"Zeke, it's worth climbing Bald Knob just to be on its summit. Besides the panoramic beauty of mountains and ridges and valleys below, there is a sense of accomplishment. A mountain doesn't look so formidable when one is standing on its top as when one is standing at its base and looking upward. If the early settlers hadn't climbed the mountains and looked down at the area about and below them, they would have discouraged and frightened them. Some of the pioneers, I've been told,

A Delightful Swimming Place, 1875

went back to the lowlands because they thought they might be forgotten at the Resurrection, if they were buried here. They never climbed the top of any of the highest mountains. Looking toward the top of a mountain from its base dismayed them and they went scrattling back, as Grandfather used to say, to the old settlements in the lowlands. There's nothing so beautiful as a mountain, Zeke. And no one so strong as a mountain man. You've heard the old saying, 'You can take a man from the mountains, but you can't take the mountains from the man.' That was meants as a slur. I turned the meaning around. It is true that the mountains can't be taken from the man. The beauty of them and the love for them that approaches adoration always remain in the heart of the mountaineer who returns to his homeland from a temporary residence in another state, 'He drank from the cold magic spring, and its waters drew him back.' Not only the pure cold water, but the scenery of the land and the friendliness of its people tugged at his heart, as the magnet draws metal."

Zeke listened attentively, but there were many words in his companion's vocabulary, which had been acquired during his absence, that he did not understand.

The driver pulled on the reins and the creaking hack stopped.

"The old swimming hole," he said.

"I want another swim," Zeke said.

So do I," echoed the other two men.

They undressed and plunged into the cold, lucid water. All good swimmers, they swam, dived, splashed water upon one another, the joyous expression of their faces being that of all swimmers, young and old, who enjoy the luxury of an old-fashioned swimming hole.

As the men were beginning to don their clothes, two newcomers sauntered down to the water's edge and began undressing. Both were barefoot and their clothing resembled that of Zeke. The taller of the men was almost the build of the mica agent.

"Hey there, Buddy!" the agent called. "How would you like to swap clothing?"

The tall stranger behaved as though he thought fun was being made of his attire.

"I mean it. Really, I'm sincere."

"Air you crazy?" asked the puzzled man.

"No, and to prove it, here's a ten-dollar bill to boot;" and he tossed the money and clothing toward the man. "Only I retain the watch and shoes."

Seated in the hack, both passengers looked similar, as to attire, but neither guessed the thoughts of the driver.

"I reckon the next time that I take these men on a trip," he told himself, "we'll be headed for the state hospital for the insane."

The vehicle jogged along the dusty, narrow road; the hackman, unaware of his actions, cracked his whip several times at the innocent horses; and the thunder of a covey of partridges, rising from the weeds by the roadside, startled the men and team for an instant.

The erstwhile buyer of mica laid his arm across Zeke's shoulders, his eyes lit, as Bald Knob loomed visibly in the distance, and he said in a voice sufficiently audible for the hackman to hear:

"When I went to the telegraph office to inform the mica company of the lease, I resigned as representative and requested that another agent be sent at its convenience. The cabin which I bought for a summer home will be my permanent residence.

"Zeke, we want to be Tuckahoes as long as we live: just happy, irresponsible Tuckahoes."

And they are still remembered by a few as two of those who participated in the past—the Then and There, so far removed from the Now and the Here.

28.
Old Superstitions

THE appearance of a comet forebodes a war.
Lightning never strikes the same spot twice.
Throw a snake into a fire and its legs will appear.
Night air is dangerous and impure.
A trip or journey should not be begun on Saturday.
Walk a crack in the floor and it will hurt your mother's back.
Walk seven cracks and it will heal your mother's back.
On Old Christmas, the bees turn over in their hives; cattle get on their knees and pray for their owners.
Handling toads will cause warts on the hands.
A baby will be born near the full moon.
Watching a person as he travels out of sight will bring bad luck to that person.
Milk from a woman's breast will cure sore eyes.
Stepping across a grave will result in the dead person's haunting one.
Naming an onion and planting it will prevent a baby's having colic.
Shingles nailed on a roof will curl, if done during the light of the moon.
Meat butchered during the decrease of the moon will shrink badly when cooked.
Chickens hatched in May will not do well.
Hogs killed on the increase of the moon will give more grease.
Dreaming of a wedding signifies the news of a death.
If an unmarried girl can't cut a pie through in a single sweep of the knife, she will die an old maid.
When your right hand itches it indicates that you will soon shake hands with a stranger.
If your left eye itches, you will soon be disappointed.
If your right eye itches, you will soon be pleased.

If you sing before breakfast, you will cry before supper.
If you sing in bed, you will lose your best friend.
If you sneeze at the table, there will be one less at the next meal.
If you cut, instead of bite, a baby's fingernails, it will grow up to be a thief.
If you clean a house before moving into it, you will never move out of it.
If you strike a child with a broom or mop, it will become a lazy adult.
Plant beans on Good Friday, unless that date comes on *blooming dates.*
Allowing a baby to see its reflection in a mirror before it is a year old will cause its death.
Naming a baby on the day of its birth will cause it to die at an early age.
Carrying a chair over a child's head will stop its growth.
A sudden ringing in the ear is a death bell for someone.
It is bad luck to kill a cat.
Seeing the new moon for the first time through green leaves is bad luck.
Twirling a chair inside the house will bring bad luck.
A hoe carried into the house will bring bad luck.
If a black cat runs across your path in front of you, turn back, for it denotes bad luck to continue the journey.
The seventh son of a seventh son and the seventh daughter of a seventh daughter have psychic powers.
Warts will soon disappear if sprinkled with dirt from a new-made grave.
A small circle of salt spread before the front door will keep witches away.
A horseshoe hung over the front door brings good fortune.
Dew swept into one's hands on a May morning, while making a wish, will cause the wish to come true.
A witch sets her broom with the brush upright.
When an unmarried girl mistakenly puts her right foot

into her left shoe, she will be married before the year ends.

To dream of a vicious dog denotes meeting a new friend.

If one can tie a knot in the fragile yellow vine, one's sweetheart dearly loves.

A splinter from a lightning-struck tree, when used as a tooth-pick, will cure an aching tooth.

When a visitor, upon leaving a home, recites the jingle, "Matthew, Mark, Luke and John, saddle the cat and I'll be gone," it denotes that she is a witch.

It is bad luck to count one's teeth.

On New Year's Day something, if only a chip of wood, should be carried into the house every time one enters it in order to have plenty during the year.

Dreaming of a naked female denotes early news of a death.

It is an omen of death for a bird to fly into the house.

A whistling girl and a crowing hen always come to a bad end.

Eat hog's jowl on New Year's Day for health and prosperity during the year.

A bee's sting denotes deceit by a friend.

The head of a buzzard tied around the neck will cure the headache.

> When Christmas is white,
> The graveyard is lean;
> But fat is the graveyard
> When Christmas is green.

Dropping an apron accidentally signifies marriage to two husbands; desertion by the husband.

A falling star signifies death.

Starching and ironing the tail of a man's shirt causes him to be harsh and quarrelsome.

Take bread when moving into a new house for good luck.

A broom falling to the floor signifies death.

A bird tapping on a window pane or shutter is a sign of death (spirit calling to spirit).

The cats should not be taken along when the family moves into another home. To do so will bring misfortune.

A cat's breath will kill a baby.

Blood poison comes more easily during dog days.

Ghosts inhabit all graveyards at night.

A white potato carried in one's pocket until it becomes stone-like will cure rheumatism.

Killing a toad will cause the cows to give bloody milk.

To tame a mule, bite its ear.

Kiss a redheaded person of the opposite sex to cure a fever blister.

A mole on the neck means money by the peck.

A horsehair placed in water will become a worm.

Ghosts appear wherever a person has been killed.

Leave a graveyard last and you will be the next person there to die.

An unmarried girl whose apron becomes wet as she washes the dishes will marry a drunkard.

The moon phases and the signs of the zodiac, when planting seeds, are very important in bringing a good crop.

Plant cucumbers before the sun rises between May 5 and 8.

Seeds planted on Good Friday bring the best crops.

If, when taking even a short trip, you must return to the house momentarily, make a cross with a stick or shoe toe in the path before turning back.

Boil a nickel or dime in water, then drink the water, to cure the hiccoughs.

Grass taken from a churchyard will cure the bite of a mad dog.

A sudden sneeze denotes news of a death.

Trimming a baby's fingernails or toenails with knife or scissors before it is a year old will cause its early death. The nails may be safely bitten with the teeth.

On New Year's Day, carry something, if only a chip of wood, into the house as often as it is entered to insure a plentiful year.

If a rooster stand in the door facing inside and crow, there will be an addition to the family during the year.
If he turn his head outside and crow, the family will lose a member before the end of the year.
When the bread burns while baking, the husband will become angry before bedtime.
A sudden sharp ringing in the ear is a death bell for a loved one.
The first corn silk seen in the spring, if red, denotes attendance at a funeral before a wedding; if white, the opposite is denoted.
If the hem of a skirt turns up in part, kissing it will cause the owner to soon get a new dress.
During a sneeze, the soul leaves the body. To insure its quick return, say, "God bless you!" to the one who sneezed.
A very intelligent child will not live to be an adult.
A man who has never seen his father can cure a baby's thrush by blowing three times in its mouth.
Dew swept into one's hands on a May morning, while making a wish will cause the wish to come true.

GOOD LUCK AND BAD LUCK SIGNS

It is the sign of bad luck for a hen to lay a very small egg.
When a black cat runs across one's path, one should return home in order to prevent bad luck.
A hoe brought into the house brings misfortune.
It is bad luck to count one's teeth.
Twirling a chair inside the house will bring bad luck, perhaps causing one's ears to drop off.
Dreaming of a nude woman is an omen of death.
Killing a cat brings certain bad luck.
Watching the new moon through green leaves brings bad luck.
When a wife accidentally drops her dishcloth, she and her husband will quarrel before bedtime.
It is an omen of death for a bird to fly into the house.

29.
Grandfather Mountain

GRANDFATHER Mountain is a dream of God molded in granite.

Its mighty peak stands under the unframed sky, sphynx-like and awe-inspiring, with a serenity born of thousands of millenniums.

It dominates a rugged stretch of lovely mountains and bonnie hills in the picturesque region of Southern Appalachia, which forms a landscape more beautiful than artist ever painted.

While eons have passed, it has been the sentinel of the Blue Ridge Mountains, rearing its head aloft to become affinity with the stars in the fields of heaven.

Whether ablaze with brightness when the sunshine mellows its features or grave in solemnity and mystery as the fog dances and fades at its base and a curtain of clouds drapes its brow, it stands as a timeless monolith which only the Creator could have fashioned.

It is abstract time become concrete majesty that mortals behold and their minds grasp more comprehensible the meaning of immortality.

It is a thing that even a pagan might view and instinctively feel that the creating Spirit called God exists at the center of the Universe.

It is a mountain which mountain folk love with a veneration that almost approaches idolatry.

It is a stupendous creation which stirs the imagination and grips the hearts of both lowlanders and mountaineers as they stand upon its summit.

It stands individualistic and aloof in the midst of other lofty peaks, including the Beech, Sugar, Roan and Mount

Mitchell, and a contour of alluring hills that sweep to the Piedmont.

With a silence that is almost audible, it says: "Behold my primitive stone that arose from the earth's interior ere the snail-paced centuries had reeled into countless eons."

At night, Grandfather Mountain, like a majestic sentinel, looms in the moonlight and the starlight, brooding in splendid loneliness above the nocturnal landscape of imposing superscenic grandeur. When day is lambent, its lightning-scarred summit, stabbing the sky, seems fit as a trysting place for archangels.

Unafraid, it watches the lightning leap from crag to crag as the angry forces of nature gather in furious array to hurl their wrath upon the exposed citadels of the highlands.

Silently it points fingers of rugged ridges to the distant Gulf of Mexico and the Atlantic Ocean that the meandering rivers which are born at its base may follow the paths to infinity.

Grandfather Mountain is dramatically resplendent when summer drapes its shoulders with an apparel of verdure and blossomy laces, giving it the odor of fern and pine needles, of balsam and rhododendron. It is gorgeous when winter has flung upon it an ermine mantle of snow, sparkling with trillions of ice-diamonds.

It is a mountain of many emotions. When viewing it at a distance, one imagines tnat it smiles in the moonlight, frowns when the shadows of evening draw their somber drapes about it, and rejoices when the valleys below are filled with birdsong. Sometimes it appears that it is a mountain of many moods, sometimes appearing as dour, morose or brooding; and again, to be genial and responsive.

Those who see Grandfather Mountain take a bit of it away in their hearts.

30.
The Answers

THOSE who would look for simple answers to the big questions should go for a country walk in the mountains on a late October afternoon, out where leaves scuffle, squirrels scurry, jays cry havoc and the fundamental shape of the hills is now revealed.

Choose a crisp leaf, no matter whether maple or oak or ash, and try to match it; and know that the leaves are almost as varied as snowflakes. Watch the wind as it turns silvery white in a clump of milkweed stalks, a shimmer of floss-borne seeds streaming from each open pod. Watch the glistening streamer from a pasture thistle's head as the wind passes, airy down full of minute flecks of fertility. See how goldenrod and asters add to the aerial cargo, and know a few of the meanings of infinity, numbers that make counting a meaningless mumble.

Hold in your hand the empty shell of a beetle or the shed husk of a locust. See the intricate parts, the ingenuity of life, now gone elsewhere, to the egg, to the pupa.

Chitin, the horny substance much like your own fingernail, but only a few weeks ago a living thing, an entity. Watch a rabbit scurry, a crow fly overhead. Look at your own hand. Know that life is more than protoplasm, more than a fertile egg ovum, that it is ultimate order in complexity.

Feel the earth underfoot. See the sky overhead. Listen to your own pulse, rhythmic as the tides. There are the answers for those who feel, and see, and listen.

31.
Early Life in The North Carolina Mountains

THE notion has been spread widely that the North Carolina Mountains were settled by inferior people and that they and their descendants for many generations were incapable of self-direction and intelligent planning, were without ambition. They have been represented as being shiftless and reckless, but an intelligent planning and leadership were evident from the beginning. Many writers from outside the mountains have painted sensational pictures of ignorance, and crime, but such views were utter foolhardiness.

Despite the handicap of geographical conditions, they made commendable progress continuously from the time of settlement. They have worked and prospered according to their environment and strong wills. In addition, they have always shown a keen interest in state and national affairs. They had more difficult problems to solve than the people who lived in more favorable environments.

The mountains were settled by families from the Piedmont Region and the Coastal Plain and from neighboring states to the north and south. Those who came were predominantly of the Anglo-Saxon strain and were self-reliant, determined and practical. There were those of Scotch-Irish, German and Welsh blood who contributed their imagination, industry and planning. The Negroes were relatively few, as the institution of slavery had little hold in the mountains. There were those who had had trouble with the royal governors; others had felt that they should escape the competition of bonded labor and the large plantation system.

For many decades, most men were hard, dogged farmers, but there were traders, hunters, cabinet makers and those of other trades. Those who worked, and most of them did, had plenty of food, clothing and comfortable homes. Unless laziness, which was rare, was a personal characteristic or illness or other misfortune came, most families fared well. Measured by financial standards, few were wealthy. Large families were the rule, not the exception, which made for a *built-in* or ready-made work force, and all members of the family who were large enough worked in the fields.

The mountaineers loved the forests and when they were not busy in their fields they spent much time among the trees, hunting, killing venomous snakes, digging ginseng, trapping, obtaining suitable timber for making tool handles, chairs, barrels, or prospecting for minerals. Regardless of his chief trade or occupation, every mountaineer was a woodsman.

Lord Byron, in a poem entitled *Daniel Boone*, described the mountain men unintentionally:

Motion was in their days, Rest in their slumbers,
   And Cheerfulness the handmaid of their toil;
Nor yet too many nor too few their numbers;
   Corruption could not make their hearts her soil;
The Lust which stings, the Splendour which encumbers,
   With the free foresters divide no spoil;
Serene, not sullen, were the solitudes
   Of this unsighing people of the woods.

Roads of their kind came early and usually followed old Indian trails, remarkable in most instances for their grades and with the badly constructed roads came the early peddler, driving a covered wagon, thus starting the barter system which lasted for many decades. These peddlers carried a variety of commodities; such as cloth, shoes, hats, notions and househould needs. These were bartered for wool, ginseng, deer hams, furs, honey and many other items. Eventually, the wagons which bartered their wares chiefly for wool became known as *wool* wagon, and these continued making their rounds for years after the Civil War had ended. So rare were wagons that they were followed and admired by both adults and children for two or three miles.

Slowly stores came into the region and the peddlers and their wagons ceased making their scheduled rounds. The first stores for decades were miles apart and these adopted the barter system because of the scarcity of money. Although the barter system for a few items still exists on a small scale in many rural stores, it mainly disappeared during the second decade of this century, although during the 'Great Depression it was resumed for several years. The items bartered at the small stores consisted chiefly of corn, beans, butter, medical roots and herbs, ginseng, wool, furs, hides, eggs, poultry, cured hams, honey and chestnuts before the blight struck.

The Civil War and its aftermath caused, so to speak, the curtain to fall for several decades, but with the determination characteristic of the mountain people, the economy was restored and improved. *Subscription* and short public schools came into being, academies were reopened and others were established. Two-week writing schools and singing schools were held in many communities; more medical doctors, though many miles apart in the rural areas, came into the region. The dauntless spirit of the people slowly triumphed.

Regional superstitions and traditions are ageless and exist in all parts of the world and the North Carolina Mountains were no exception. As time passed and social intercourse with the outside world and with those from outside the mountains increased; with the coming of better schools, colleges, libraries, newspapers and magazines, most of the colorful beliefs and traditions have been discarded or forgotten. The greatest value of remembering them at all is to become acquainted with a part, at least, of the rich folklore that once existed and were once accepted by many persons of the mountains as scientific truths.

32.
The Anthology of Death

JACOB *(Uncle Jake)* Carpenter, born in 1833 on Three Mile Creek in what is now Avery County, scrawled down in his notebooks a unique record which later generations called his *Anthology of Death*. The following excerpts, spelling and syntax unchanged, are given from his old writings, no effort having been made to keep them in sequence:

Davis Frank ag 72 dide july 29 1842 ware fin man but mad sum brandy that warnt no good

Wm Carpenter ag 76 dide nov 15 1881 war fin honter cild bar and wolf by 100 der by 100

Abern Johnson ag 100.7 dide july 2 he war farmer and run forg to mak iron and drunk likker all his days

Hargon Olles ag 83 jun 11 dide he war farmer and great liar

Alek Wiseman ag 80 march 20 1877 ware a good man to make brandy

John Clark ag 42 dide july 14 1914 from milk sick no brandy

Boon Pratt ag 28 dide sep 7 1906 work hard all life got rattel snak bite brandy cured it

Wm Gary age 96 dide jan 2 1894 ware der honter and bar honter cild 200 bar 100 dere

Frise Stamey ag 63 jan 9 1914 dide. Ware good shristen woman. She had 12 children

Charles McKinney ag 79 dide may 1852 ware a farmer lived in blew ridge had 4 womin married 1 live in McKinney gap all went to fields to mak grane all went to crib for corn all went to smok house for meat he cild 75 to 80 hoges a year and womin never had no words bout his havin so many womin if it war thes times thar would be har pulled thare ware 42 children belongin to him they all went to prechin together nothin said he mad brandy all his lif never had no foes got along fin with everibody nod him

Wm. Davis ag 100.8 dide october 5 1841 war old sojer in rev war an mad brandy an never had no dronkards in famely

Samuel Frank ag 94 dide july 12 1857 he wars farmer hwed logs for hoses no man cod bete him

Turner carpenter ag 23 dide nov 10 1862 he fot for his contry loste lif

Josef Pyatt a 75 jan 15 dide 1864 he wars farmer mad hoges by 100

Pegey Wise a 75 dide oc 15 1868 she wars granny womin for contry.

Soonsy Olles ag 84 dide june 10 1871 grates Dere honter & turkies bee trees by honders and ratel snak by 100 dere by thousan

henery barrier ag 78 dide march 15 1871 was fin honter cil bar by 100

Peg Chatem ag 72 dide auges 14 1886 she spon an wove cloth

Kim Kone ag 75 dide oc 15 1888 wars blacksmith he had 6 gals tha cod work in shop tha wars 6 feet hi

Margit Carpenter ag 87 dide jun 5 1876 wars good womin good for pore she did not have no bed to slep on when she wars marid she slep on dereskin til marid but that look like hard times no womin had to lie on dereskin when marid

Dock Chiles ag 82 di march 5 1859 wars docker

The last entry *Uncle Jake* made in his notebood reads: "Jacob Carpenter is sick took bed this day." He died on March 10, 1920.

33.
Why Not Come Over and Borrow?

SINCE the beginnings of borrowings among neighbors, there's always been the broad hint, if not suspicion, that these backyard, backdoor visits were more for the passing of the time of day or tidbits of gossip, than for the purpose of fetching a cup of sugar.

In fact, few of those neighborly minglings ever produced any really substantial loans. Perhaps, a dollop of shortening for the dinner biscuits until the borrower could get to the store, maybe a couple of eggs for the upside-down cake until the hens came through, or even a spool of thread.

Never anything important enough to cause next-door neighbors to fall out because of non-repayments.

Those back-door visits, really, were just homey little chats during which folks who lived next door or nearby could get to know each other better.

Maybe, this is why there are so many strangers these days: neighbors don't drop over any more to borrow cups of sugar.

—*Wilmington, N. C. Star.*

34.
Colorful Place-Names

MANY communities and villages of the North Carolina Mountains have colorful names which they received from folklore relating or pertaining to the area. Following is a list of a few of them and the names of the counties in which they are located:

Bamboo, Watauga
Bandanna, Mitchell
Bearpaw, Cherokee
Bearwallow, Henderson
Bible, Madison
Bethel, Haywood
Birdtown, Swain
Briertown, Macon
Cattail Creek, Yancey
Chickentown, Avery
Cottonpatch, Haywood
Cranberry, Avery
Democrat, Buncombe
Friendship, Cherokee
Hawk, Mitchell
Hardscrabble, Yancey
High Rock City, Avery
Hidetown, Graham
Hanging Dog, Cherokee
Horseshoe, Henderson

Ledger, Mitchell
Lick Log, Avery; Burke
Lickskillet
Loafers Glory, Mitchell; Buncombe
Memory, Avery
Needmore, Swain
Plumtree, Avery
Pumpkintown, Jackson
Relief, Mitchell
Senia, Avery
Spear, Avery
Shooting Creek, Clay
Spruce Pine, Mitchell
Suits, Cherokee
Three Mile, Avery
Uno, Henderson
Vests, Cherokee
Whaley, Avery

35.
Funny Incidents

SHE CERTAINLY WAS

AT the turn of the century at a little church in a remote settlement of the mountains, an old preacher, ending a funeral sermon of a deceased member of his church, the mother of 14 children, said: "She was a kind neighbor, a devoted Christian, a trustworthy wife, a wonderful mother—and, Lord, what a breeder!"

HE TRIED TO FLY TO HEAVEN

In the summer of 1905, John Elisha, an old Negro preacher whose Christianity appeared more real than his general knowledge, announced to his wife and children that he intended flying to heaven on a pair of turkey wings the next day.

The next day around mid-morning, he dressed himself in his Sunday-go-to-meeting clothes which he had recently purchased at the C. W. Burleson Store, Plumtree, took his pressed and dried turkey wings, and climbed to the roof of his low log cabin. After bidding his weeping wife and children goodbye, he ran the length of the roof, fanning the air with the turkey wings—and fell upon a pile of ashes from the fireplace, not badly hurt.

THE PUREBRED CHICKENS

An old man whose given name was Leffler, a descendant of Pennsylvania Dutch and who died in what was then a part of Mitchell County during the last half of the Nineteenth Century, was known for his exaggerations and telling some of his tales without sufficient thought, told this one:

Grist mill with an overshot wheel

"Several years ago, seeing an advertisement in a newspaper offering purebred Plymouth Rock eggs for sale, I ordered twelve. Only five of the eggs hatched, half being roosters and half pullets. When dem chickens growed up, they mated just like ganders and geese."

A LEAP TO SAFETY

In 1905, a rather severe windstorm struck Lick Log Gap, a Negro settlement near Frank, and blew the low log cabin partly from its stone pillars and twisting the hinges of the door to the extent that it could not be opened sufficiently for exit of the family inside, but the very low chimney was not affected.

The badly frightened mother and her six children ran up the inside of the chimney and jumped to the ground, thus escaping safely.

36.

With Love to Beautiful Western North Carolina

THE things I like best about Western North Carolina include:

The friendly and hospitable people.

The Great Smoky Mountains, Mount Mitchell, the Big Yellow Mountain, Grandfather Mountain and Beech Mountain.

Handicrafts, folk music and square dancing.

The French Broad River.

The good highways, the crooked secondary roads and the bridle paths across the mountains.

Ham gravy at Appalachian Inn in Minneapolis.

The Brown Mountain Lights and Linville Caverns.

Black loam soil, home gardens and apple orchards.

The Blue Ridge Parkway.

Appalachian State University; State University, Asheville; Mars Hill College, and West Carolina University.

The memory and graves of Zebulon Vance, O. Henry, Locke Craig and Thomas Wolfe.

The gorgeous mountain colors in October.

The goldenrod and wild blue asters in the fall.

Biltmore House.

Tweetsie Railroad and the Land of Oz.

Maggie Valley and Ghost Mountain.

The Cherokee Indian Reservation.

The *giving of tongues* by the hounds in a fox chase.

Such beautiful and ugly names Watauga, Swannanoa, Hiawassee, Cheowah, Nantahala, Beaucatcher, Sandy Mush, Big Horse, Hump, Hominy, and Spivy.

Linville Gorge, Table Rock and Hawkbill.

A View from the Top of Paint Rock, 1875

Names like Lick Log Gap, Saxapaw, Howard's Knob, Casar, Devil's Race Path Branch, Cow Camp, Scaly, Cattail Creek, Blood Camp and Short Off Mountain.
Picnic tables and camp grounds.
Sunset and moonrise from a mountain top.
The Blue Ridge.
Penland School of Handicrafts.
The many churches and schools, that dot the mountain region.

A Wildly Beautiful River Valley, 1875

37.
I Want to Go Back

I WANT to go back to the mountains. The change would be sweet emotions to my heart. Here the land is all covered with bricks and concrete and the hearts of many of the people are as hard and flinty as the sidewalks.

Yes, I want to go back to the country, where the air is soft and pure; where the neighbors will come in, *set up* with the sick and help dig a grave and shovel the dirt on their departed friends, dropping a genuine tear of regrets at their passing; where they go to *meeting* and *pitch* the tune with tuning forks and sing with the fervor and spirit of the faithful and where all church services were at *early candlelight*, if they were not at night.

I want to trim the lamp wicks again and fill the lamps with oil carried from a country store in a can with an Irish *tater* stuck in the spout. I want to eat sweet *taters* baked in an oven on the *heath* over hickory and red oak coals. I want to see the small boy swing the flybrush to keep the flies *offen* the food on the dining table.

I want to go back where all the common, everyday towels were made of flour sacks and where there was only one store towel which was put out when the preacher came. I want to see the man of the house take his table knife of chilled steel and whet it on the fork tines before he carved the meat that had been cooked with the beans.

If you've never eaten any lye hominy or shuck beans, you never have really lived.

I want to go back where they make sausage and souse meat, where the pumpkin is sliced and hung on quilting frames to dry. (That was before germs, vitamins and termites had been invited.) I want to carry the old Barlowe knife once more and whittle red cedar and soft poplar.

I want to see the housewife reach into the salt gourd and get a pinch or two of salt to season the beans and taters and who has not seen the *saft* soap put in a terrapin's shell, with Grandpa's initials cut on the side.

I want to go into the *bighouse* and set by the fire and see the old-fashioned dog irons, the wrought iron shovel and tongs, made in the country blacksmith shop. I want to watch Pa heat the old shovel on a bitter cold day and hold it in front of the old Seth Thomas clock to thaw out the frozen oil so the old timepiece could go on ticking off the hours. I want to see the old sunmarks on the back door sill when they had no clocks or the clocks they had were unreliable. There was no such thing then as daylight saving time. They got up at three o'clock in the morning and went to bed at seven, unless it was applebutter making time, when they remained up until around eight.

The *parlor* was the sacred place. There was where all the *sparking* was done; there was the bed—and what a bed!—the preacher slept in when he visited the family. The bed had two straw *ticks*, a big featherbed and a bolster and two large feather pillows. When the bed was not in use, the pillows were covered by *shams* which had mottoes *worked on* them.

On the *center table* was the old family album with plush backs which held the pictures of the family, some of them dating back to the Civil War. These old tintypes sometimes showed the likenesses of distant relatives who had fought with Scott in Mexico. Those in civilian clothes always had one hand on the knee and the other spread on the stomach.

I want to go back where all the shoe boxes were saved to make splints for the women's and girls' bonnets which were shaped like half-barrels with *tails* to cover the necks.

I want to spend Christmas in the country and get off the Christmas tree one stick of candy, one orange and one penny pencil.

I want to get back where the geese and ducks are picked, where the corn is planted by hand and soup is made by the signs of the moon; where walnuts and hickory nuts are gathered in the fall for the winter mast; where roots and herbs are gathered for medicine for the sick; where the pegging awl is still in use; where green coffee grains are parched in the stove and ground in a mill hung on the kitchen wall or held between the knees.

Yes, I want to go back where they drink sassafras tea to thin their blood in the springtime; where they churn with the old up-and-down churn; where they turn the cream jar around as it sits by the fireplace in the *big house* so it will get in the right *kelter* for churning; where they always lick their knives before they cut butter; where goose quill toothpicks are still in use; where they still *battle* the clothes on washday; where they fill the straw-ticks after thrashing time and cord the beds every month; where they wear their flannel underwear and the younger children wear bibs at mealtime.

Yes, I want to go back to the mountains and get my fill of crackling bread; I want to see the old whatnot in the corner of the *bighouse;* I want to engage in a spelling match in Webster's old blueback spelling book and read from McGuffey's Reader; I want to see the schoolchildren in the one-room schoolhouse, one after another, raise their hands and say, "Teacher, may I go outdoors?"

I want to see the people eat again and shovel it in with their knives; I want to borrow a neighbor's gimlet; I want to go back where they eat three meals a day — breakfast, dinner and supper, and where the word *lunch* will never be heard again.

I want to go back and make another *cornshucker* from locust wood.

I want to go to the cane patch, strip the blades off some cane, top it and haul it to the cane mill, then skim the *skimmings* off the boiling molasses.

I want to go to a neighbor's house to get the free seed corn for which he never charges another neighbor.

Mountain farmers gather in Asheville, 1890

I want to pull out the old trundlebed and sleep the sleep of the just once more.

I would like to call a few doodle bugs *outen* their holes.

I want to avoid the Spanish needles, the cockle burrs, the seed ticks, the beggar lice and the chiggers that make life unbearable.

I'd like to see the old sidesaddle hanging on a peg in the wall of the front porch, covered by a sateen riding skirt.

I want to prime the ash hopper again.

I want to get a sassafras stick to stir the boiling homemade soap.

Yes, I want to go back!

—*Tri-County News*, Spruce Pine.

Plowing time and Jackson Franklin was ready.

Jonas Ridge Store and Church

Young Farmers

Plowing time and Jackson Franklin was ready.

Jonas Ridge Store and Church

Young Farmers

A One-room School

Large Families were once in order.

A buggy was a dream come true.

A One-room School

Large Families were once in order.

A buggy was a dream come true.

"Revenoor" Stokes Penland raids an early moonshine still

State law once required all men between ages of 21 and 45 to furnish their own tools and work four days free labor annually on county roads.

A Portable Sawmill

"Revenoor" Stokes Penland raids an early moonshine still

State law once required all men between ages of 21 and 45 to furnish their own tools and work four days free labor annually on county roads.

A Portable Sawmill

Off for a Hayride

One Sunday afternoon

A Corn Shucking

Off for a Hayride

One Sunday afternoon

A Corn Shucking

DATE DUE